A Manual of

Archival Techniques

Roland M. Baumann, Editor

Commonwealth of Pennsylvania

**PENNSYLVANIA HISTORICAL
AND MUSEUM COMMISSION**

Harrisburg, 1979

Contents

APPENDIXES

Introduction

PLANS for the Pennsylvania Historical and Museum Commission to sponsor a series of archival techniques workshops to be held in the Commonwealth in 1978 were broached by Executive Director William J. Wewer in the fall of 1976. The purpose of the project was to improve the process of preserving the valuable historical records in Pennsylvania. The staff of the Commission's Bureau of Archives and History was asked to prepare a grant proposal to an appropriate funding agency. Since the project's principal objective was the dissemination of techniques related to the preservation and use of historical records, support was sought from the National Historical Publications and Records Commission (NHPRC). In line with NHPRC records program guidelines, the proposal was submitted to the State Historical Records Advisory Board for its consideration and for its approval, which was given on February 22, 1977. The proposal was then approved by the NHPRC at its November, 1977, board meeting. The three workshops on archival techniques were held in 1978 at Harrisburg (May 19), Pittsburgh (June 9) and Wilkes-Barre (September 15). The institutional hosts were, respectively, the Pennsylvania Historical and Museum Commission, the Historical Society of Western Pennsylvania, and the Wyoming Historical and Geological Society.

The Commonwealth was divided into three regions, with a third of the counties invited to and a majority of them represented at each workshop. Brought together for the first time on a systematic basis were local historical societies and archival units affiliated with colleges, universities and religious denominations. Thus, the focus was on assisting organizations, both large and small, that have traditionally amassed much historical material, but have lacked professional staff and financial resources to carry on even a modest archives program. The goal to improve the preservation of records was for the most part, we believe, successful. Some 225 individuals participated in the workshops, which combined topical presentations of established and proven approaches and practical demonstrations.

A Manual of Archival Techniques is a by-product of the workshops. Although a publication was included in the original grant proposal, it was uncertain what type of publication would result from the project. But, as we listened to the papers and the remarks of our distinguished experts on historical administration and manuscript preparation and preservation, we concluded that their contributions were eminently worthy of publication. The faculty was asked to address itself to the problems of local historical societies, and to provide ground-level techniques and inexpensive solutions to them. This its members have done. Therefore, we feel fortunate in having the opportunity to print their presentations, because we can now reach not only the participants a second time but also distribute this *Manual* to the many manuscript curators, archivists and historical society volunteers who were not able to attend one of these three workshops.

Roland M. Baumann, *Chief*
DIVISION OF ARCHIVES AND MANUSCRIPTS

Acknowledgments

We are indebted to many persons who have made these workshops and this publication of the Pennsylvania Historical and Museum Commission possible. Acknowledgment is due to the National Historical Publications and Records Commission, whose grant of $5,950 in December, 1977, provided for full support of the workshops and partial support of the *Manual*. The Pennsylvania Federation of Historical Societies provided assistance in handling publicity and promotion of these workshops. We also wish to give special thanks to the members of the Pennsylvania Historical and Museum Commission and its Executive Director, William J. Wewer, for approving this publication. Harry E. Whipkey, Director, Bureau of Archives and History; Roland M. Baumann, Chief, Division of Archives and Manuscripts; and John E. Bodnar, Chief, Division of History, were involved in this project from the beginning. Mr. Whipkey served as project director and Drs. Baumann and Bodnar as associate project directors. Harold L. Myers, Associate Historian, guided and supervised the editorial and printing arrangements. Mrs. Deborah Miller, Miss Angela M. Orsini and Mrs. Dorothy Weiser provided typing and clerical services for the project as needed. To all these people and to others who have not been named we express our gratitude.

CONTRIBUTORS

Roland M. Baumann, Chief, Division of Archives and Manuscripts, Pennsylvania Historical and Museum Commission

Edmund Berkeley, Jr., Curator of Manuscripts, Alderman Library, University of Virginia

Elisabeth W. Betz, Picture Cataloging Specialist, Prints and Photographs Division, Library of Congress

George Chalou, Archivist Supervisor, National Archives

Jeffrey Field, Program Officer, Center for Research Programs, Division of Research Grants, National Endowment for the Humanities

William Fraley, Assistant Executive Director, National Historical Publications and Records Commission

Jean Gunner, Bookbinder/Conservator, Hunt Institute, Carnegie-Mellon University

Norvell Jones, Paper Conservator, Preservation Office, Library of Congress

Samuel Mauray, Manager, State Records Center, Pennsylvania Historical and Museum Commission

Peter J. Parker, Chief of Manuscripts, Historical Society of Pennsylvania

Willman Spawn, Conservator, American Philosophical Society

William Schneider, Associate Director for Research and Evaluation, Pennsylvania Committee for the Humanities

Gail Stern, Associate Director for Program Management, Pennsylvania Committee for the Humanities

Leon J. Stout, Head, Penn State Room, Pattee Library, Pennsylvania State University

Frank M. Suran, Associate Archivist, Division of Archives and Manuscripts, Pennsylvania Historical and Museum Commission

Harry E. Whipkey, State Archivist and Director, Bureau of Archives and History, Pennsylvania Historical and Museum Commission

Frank Zabrosky, Curator, Archives of Industrial Society, University of Pittsburgh

Part 1

THE ADMINISTRATION OF HISTORICAL RECORDS

An Overview

The Historical Setting

By Peter J. Parker

WHEN I was first asked to speak to these workshops about the administration of archives and manuscripts, I naively thought that the task would be an easy one: all I would have to do would be to describe the operations of my own shop. However, even if you were to forgive my vanity, I doubt that you would have forgiven the disjointed text that I would have produced. I realized that I had never really thought out just what it is that archival administrators really do. Once I had begun that process of self-examination, I discovered a great many shortcomings in my own shop and in my thinking. So, if what follows seems unduly admonitory, please remember that these are the words of a repentant sinner.

Administration is the art of making things work, or, if you will, the achievement of what is necessary by the manipulation of the possible. Creating the appropriate setting for the administration of archives requires that one learn what is possible. To do that we must come to terms with the realities that determine how—and with what—we do our jobs. To illustrate these realities, and to give this discussion some substance, let us posit the existence of the Yahoo County Historical Society (YCHS), an organization founded in 1867 and now housed in an old bank building that the society acquired in 1934. The collections run the gamut from manuscript deed books, deposited at the society in 1937 by the county clerk in flagrant disregard of the Commonwealth's public records acts, to photographs, tools, old letters, an ante-bellum wedding dress, furniture, more letters and some account books. In fact, the historical society is the attic of Yahoo County, even to the details of arrangement and odors.

Let us further assume that the board of directors of YCHS has decided to clean out this attic and has hired a professional archivist to do the job. However, before this Intrepid Archivist sets to work with brooms and trash compactor, he had better take stock of the realities that he will face at YCHS: What purpose does the society serve? Who governs it? What is the source of funds? And, finally, how has YCHS defined the archivist's job?

Some of the answers to these questions will be found in the YCHS constitution, its board minutes, its financial statements. Yet, if YCHS is anything like the Historical Society of Pennsylvania, the constitution will be high-sounding and vague, the minutes tantalizingly incomplete, and the funds insufficient. But this is necessary homework if the archivist is to discover just how much maneuvering room he really has.

Next, the archivist should find out who uses the society. And, more important, does YCHS have the potential to serve a larger, more diversified public? The relationship between the society's constituency and its funding is too obvious to need elaboration; indeed, almost every foundation and endowment application asks, "How many people will benefit?" But it is not simply numbers that count. How well is the public served? And, do the people of Yahoo County have confidence that the society will be able to deliver what is needed now and ten years from now?

The reasons for taking stock of the society's purpose and its public are clear: within the limits permitted, the archivist must work to create in Yahoo County an atmosphere of trust and the expectation of continuity. To that end, he should examine the society's rules, its operating policies and procedures. If they are fair to the public and curatorially responsible — admittedly sometimes a difficult balance to achieve — they should be publicized. If they are not fair or responsible, they should be revised in consultation with the society's director and its board. Access rules, for example, should be as nonrestrictive as possible and they ought to be in writing. Special restrictions about photocopying ought to be posted, too. In short, the archivist should insure that everyone believes he is being treated even-handedly at YCHS. Although YCHS may be privately funded, its tax-exempt status derives from its continuing service to the public.

Public service is only one of the factors that will insure public support. Clearly, people will come to YCHS because of the quality of its collections. The society has what they can get nowhere else. There is nothing that the archivist can do about the vigor or lassitude with which his predecessors pursued the society's mandate; he can, however, insure that he understands that mandate and fulfills it as best he can. He can insure that the collections already on the shelves are arranged, described, properly housed and well cared for. He should organize the mess that is in the attic and see to it that these "new" collections are equally well cared for. Finally, he should look for new material that reinforces the strengths of the collections at YCHS. Such are the attributes of stewardship.

Successful stewardship is the product of an odd concatenation of qualities that I hope all archivists and curators possess in some measure: respect for the immense variety of human life, an awareness of how records reflect that variety, and a natural curiosity about all manner of things from copyright to collecting policies, from air conditioning to the geology of Yahoo County. But awareness and curiosity are effective qualities only if the archivist knows what he is doing. And that, of course, is the purpose of the papers that follow. The authors will point to specific solutions for particular problems; they will touch upon only a few of our professional skills. The rest the archivist must nose out for himself. A good place to start is the Basic Manual Series, published by the Society of American Archivists in 1977, and the bibliography compiled by Frank Evans, cited below.

I suggested above that one of the archivist's responsibilities is to insure that the collections are well housed and cared for. To do this I believe that the archivist should first look at the physical plant of YCHS. How consistent is the atmosphere? Which radiators leak? Where is the fuse box and how good is the wiring? Again, the society's archives may provide some of the answers. A good set of plans for the building is invaluable. So, too, is a good set of records which, if not already maintained by the building superintendent, the archivist ought to begin. Without such records it would be very difficult for the archivist to justify double-glazing or even air conditioning the stacks or public spaces. The utility of such records should become so self-evident to the superintendent that he will want to take them over!

One of the most telling measures of stewardship is how well the archivist knows his collections—not only what is on the shelves of YCHS, but also what is *not*. If inventories and descriptions exist for some or all of the collections, they will furnish the essential "who, what, where and when"; but there is no substitute for processing in learning what is contained in a collection. In many cases, however, the archivist will be faced with the detritus of past generations of processing. Because YCHS was founded in 1867, and because its early members were probably interested in genealogical materials, the collections that came in the earlier years were probably item-catalogued and may even have been arranged alphabetically. Indeed, the tendency to do this was probably encouraged by the professional training of the early librarians who administered the collection: they tended to think of each document as a discrete bibliographical entity. But once new collections arrived they began to realize how staggering was the task that they had begun. And so the backlog began.

When collections are broken up, or remain unprocessed, notes on provenance disappear. For collections already on the shelves and those in the attic, the archivist will have to resort once again to the YCHS board minutes. Perhaps, too, the bulletins issued to members might answer. But the game is worth the candle: notes on provenance, or the origin and history of ownership of a collection, are valuable research tools in their own right. They permit the archivist and researcher to fit together pieces they might not otherwise have recognized as coming from the same puzzle.

For collections just arriving, the archivist ought to secure all the information he can about the materials at the time of transfer. In particular, the archivist ought to learn whether the donor or the office of origin has removed any materials from the collection. Fugitive or alienated materials may come on the market in later years; it would be useful to know where they came from.

Provenance notes are only one of the tools by which the archivist learns about his collection. They form the basis for the collection file, the *omnium gatherum* of information about each collection. Additionally the file should contain correspondence and a copy of the deed of gift or deposit agreement, a list of materials removed from the collection at the time of processing, publication history, copies of inventories or registers, and even the curator's notes about the research done on the collection. The collection file is the archivist's basic tool; it need not be generally available to the public.

Because the public in Yahoo County probably still looks upon YCHS as an attic into which things may be put or from which they may be withdrawn at whim, the archivist is going to have to educate his director and the public to the advantages of an orderly transfer of title to the materials received. One should attempt to get a written instrument of transfer from each donor containing (1) transfer of legal title of the materials to YCHS, (2) permission for YCHS to sell, exchange, or destroy unwanted materials (unless, of course, the donor wishes to have them returned), (3) the specific transfer of whatever literary rights the donor may have had in the materials to YCHS.

Few institutions are now accepting deposits. If, however, they are necessary, the terms should be spelled out in writing. It might be wise, for example, to insure that YCHS recover processing and storage costs if the materials are removed. (Appended are a sample deed of gift and a sample deposit agreement, Appendix I.)

The archivist will soon come to know the strengths and weaknesses of the collections at YCHS and how these collections relate one to another. If, for example, the society holds Adam Sitzplatz's field notes for the original surveys of the county, is there a collection of maps or plats keyed to the Sitzplatz surveys? Or, perhaps the plats are at the public library. If so, the archivist will have to decide whether to use the meagre resources of YCHS to assemble a set of copies.

The archivist must know how much of the available universe of information about the county YCHS holds. Of what does that universe consist? Only a thorough knowledge of the county's history can answer that: industry, settlement patterns, and agricultural development are all as important as the county's political history as subjects to be documented. If that documentation is not at YCHS, where is it? To find out, the archivist should visit nearby institutions. Perhaps he and his colleagues can make a concerted effort to recapture more of that universe.

The society's collections, whether new or old, must be kept secure. To that end, the archivist must insure that the staff is ever-watchful. Patrons should be continually aware of a high-security profile; they should be made to believe that the staff has complete object control over the YCHS collections. Common sense measures will suggest themselves, especially after reading Tim Walch on "Security" in the Basic Manual Series; but it is well to remember that security is a state of mind.

Central to any security program is an awareness of the public who uses the resources of YCHS. Readers ought to fill out an application to use the collections or leave some other record of their research (Appendix II). Once the completed application is in hand, the archivist ought to talk with the reader at some length. The interview serves both security and reference functions; it gives the archivist the chance to show the reader the ropes while letting him know the rules. And, finally, the conversation will give the archivist the opportunity to make that sensitive judgment we all must make: whether the reader can be trusted with unique archival materials.

Fortunately, we see few researchers who cannot be trusted. Most will be grateful for the reference help and for familiarization with the rules. But the archivist will be in a much stronger position with the "difficult" reader if all of the important rules are in writing and are posted (Appendix II). Needless to say, the rest of the staff should be equally familiar with the society's operating procedures.

But, YCHS is not in business to thwart legitimate research. The interview gives the archivist the opportunity to assist the reader in getting to important materials while steering him away from low-yield collections. This saves manuscripts from needless handling while saving the reader time.

It is important, too, that during the initial interview the reader learn the society's photocopying rules and procedures. Not only does the new copyright statute bear upon these procedures, but good stewardship requires that one be very selective about what may be copied. Patrons should not be permitted to make xerographic copies for themselves. And, I suggest, copying charges ought to be set sufficiently high to discourage indiscriminate copying. Alternatively, some numerical limit may be set on the number of pages copied for each patron each day.

Because manscripts, like rare books, may be damaged by xerography, it may be necessary for YCHS to provide microfilming services. Few societies can afford a camera and operator, so perhaps YCHS will have to explore the pros and cons of a service bureau. But one ought to keep in mind that a service bureau may damage manuscripts more than in-house xerography. One solution may be to permit the reader to make his own copies, using a hand-held camera with available light.

No matter how photocopies are produced, the archivist should know what has been copied. Obviously, he cannot record each xerographic copy, but if YCHS films an entire collection or bibliographical entity and retains the negative, the archivist should note it in the appropriate collection file. And, every copy that leaves YCHS should bear both a copyright warning and a notice that permission for reproduction must be secured in writing from the society.

A last word on photocopying: policies that are too restrictive may encourage theft; one should make some provision for copying.

The prospect of theft offends and frightens us all. Readers, staff and volunteers are all potential felons. One must presume that YCHS has looked into the backgrounds of its staff and volunteers. The interview, however, is probably not enought to permit a considered judgment about a reader's integrity. Hence, one should have some record of all materials that each reader uses. Request slips should be as precise as possible and should be kept even after material has been returned. Some institutions require that request slips be placed on the shelf or in the container from which materials have been removed. They also require that the person refiling materials initial the call slips as he refiles. Other institutions use the reader's application as a request slip, thereby limiting the reader to one volume or one item at a time. However, no matter what method one adopts, it has got to be simple and easily understood by readers and staff alike. And it has to be consistently applied, for security should be more than a state of mind; it should be a habit.

I am afraid that for most of us conservation can be little more than a state of mind. Few institutions can afford a conservator or a binder. An increasing number of regional conservation centers may offer a partial solution, but the problem of conservation will always fall primarily upon the curator/archivist. Not only must he determine what is to be repaired, but he must also maintain the collections in the best condition he can.

The archivist can train himself to minimize damage to the collections by following certain common-sense procedures. Mould, vermin and bugs can be controlled by good housekeeping. Neither staff nor patrons should eat or drink except in authorized areas, remote from storage spaces. Awareness of the environment and simple ingenuity can do much to minimize the extremes of heat, humidity and light that are so damaging to collections. One might consider, for example, painting the windows that face south and west; it is certainly cheaper than air conditioning.

There are many other measures one can take to stabilize collections. Proper storage in acid-free materials, such as those sold by the Hollinger Corporation, will retard (or at least not accelerate) acid deterioration. Adequate shelving will reduce physical damage to archival materials. And, of course, throughtfully worked out photocopying procedures will further reduce damage to the collections. Finally, the archivist must work to make the entire staff at YCHS conservation- conscious.

To what end have these remarks been directed? I have attempted to provide an essential attitudinal framework for the papers that follow. I have attempted, too, to suggest that as our fictitious Intrepid Archivist takes up his responsibilities at the YCHS, he will put on a coat of many colors, a seamless garment. There really can be no job description for what he does; he is simply a steward.

But successful stewardship is not necessarily passive. Keep in mind the parable of the talents: the archivist should not bury his talent. He should be visible. He should continually keep his director informed of what he is doing. He should offer advice to readers and be ready to offer it to his colleagues, should they ask. He should seek speaking engagements and should court potential donors. From his knowledge of the collections at YCHS, as well as those at nearby institutions, he should set out the guidelines for an institutional collecting policy. He should draft a statement about the society's collecting policies, and after clearing it with the director, see to it that it is published and circulated to other institutions. And the archivist might consider formal cooperation with sister institutions to create a regional collecting network.

First, however, our Intrepid Archivist must put his own house in order and clean out the attic of Yahoo County. The papers that follow will help him do that job well.

Part 2

ARCHIVAL METHODOLOGY

Arrangement of Archives
and Manuscripts

Appraisal and Arrangement
Of Textual Records

By Frank A. Zabrosky

WAYNE C. GROVER, archivist of the United States from 1948 to 1965, in developing his "Archivist's Code," offered this proposition as part of the code:

> The Archivist in appraising records for retention or disposal acts as the agent of future generations. The wisdom and impartiality he applies to this task measure his professionalism, for he must be as intelligent in disposing of records that have no significant or lasting value as in retaining those that do.

With the responsibility of appraisal goes the obligation to make the historical records available and accessible by arranging and describing the materials. The problems of appraisal and arrangement are complex, as perplexing at times to the experienced practitioner as to the neophyte.

This essay will summarize the principles, methodology and techniques which govern these two aspects of archival/manuscript work. In preparing this essay, I have drawn heavily on two new invaluable works prepared under the auspices of the Society of American Archivists: Maynard J. Brichford's *Archives and Manuscript Appraisal and Accessioning* (Chicago, 1977) and David B. Gracy II's *Archives and Manuscripts: Arrangement and Description* (Chicago, 1977). Any lack of clarity which may surface is mine and not that of Brichford and Gracy, the authors of the manuals.

In analyzing the problems of appraisal and arrangement faced by administrators of public records, e.g., records managers, archivists and manuscript curators, it is apparent that although there is a mutuality in methodology and technique, the differences in origin and ultimate purpose of historical records agencies require some variation in treatment. How records are appraised and arranged in governmental archives, for example, differs somewhat and, at times, ambiguously from the methodology and techniques employed by private historical records agencies. It is to be hoped that this paper will point out and reconcile the areas of difference.

11

APPRAISAL

The Committee on Terminology of the Society of American Archivists has defined appraisal as

> the process of determining the value and, thus, the disposition of records based upon their current administrative, legal, and fiscal use; their evidential and informational or research value; their arrangement and their relationship to other records.

Appraisal is one of the areas of greatest challenge to the archivist/curator. He must understand the past, develop a perspective as to the future, and analyze which documentation relating to an organization or to an individual will be of enduring historical value, and merit retention and preservation in an archives or historical repository.

The archivist/curator must consider the entire organization he serves, weighing the importance of its activities against the resources it can devote to its archival/manuscript program, and considering its relationship to other institutions—adjacent, regional or far—which have similar programs. An essential consideration is the collection's subject relevance to existing holdings within the institution and whether the material in the collection would extend current research strengths, interests and needs in a logical manner while anticipating future research needs.

Records appraisal is a process by which one makes a thorough analysis of the origins, characteristics and attributes, both physical and substantive, of records; a knowledge of techniques for the segregation and selection of records; an awareness of the development of research methodologies and needs; and a consideration of administrative, research and archival values.

Characteristics of Records

The archivist/curator, when appraising records, will study their age, volume and form and will analyze their functional, evidential and informational value.

Many disasters, man-made as well as natural, such as floods, fires and inadequate care, have caused time gaps in records. The absence of other prime documents for a period causes the appraiser to keep records which might ordinarily be destroyed. Adequacy of other documentation for understanding past historical periods is an important consideration when selecting records, particularly when large volume and bulk are involved. Records appear in a myriad of forms: official records, personal papers, printed archives and publications, photographs, sound recordings, film, and machine-readable tapes; each form inherently has individual characteristics which must guide appraisal. Frequently, the most valuable records are those dealing with policies, programs and reports. Photographs over an extended time period provide cumulative value. Large quantities of data of long-term value are reducible through magnetic tape storage, but such material has to be judged in relation to record content, related textual material, available programs, and accessible software, e.g., computer models, terminals, etc.

The intrinsic values of records, that is their functional, evidential and informational content, basically determine appraisal. Each record was created to perform a function — personal letter, ledger, check. Some functional categories are usually valuable and worth preserving — diaries, minutes, organizational charts; some are not — cancelled checks. One, however, must exercise caution and judgment and not let form belie substance. For instance, at the Archives of Industrial Society, there is a manuscript group containing the records of the Pittsburgh Symphony Society with a series of cancelled checks. Before these checks are discarded, it might be prudent to review them for signatures of noted personalities. Obviously, this would be done only if one felt that the particular instance warranted expenditure of staff time or utilization of space.

Records contain evidence of the "organization, functions, policies, decisions, procedures, operations and other activities" of the office that produced them. Agency histories, directories, speeches, legal opinions and such records which demonstrate performance at various levels of the managerial, supervisory and work processes are valuable. Most records contain factual data about the persons, corporate bodies, events and problems with which they deal. An institution's purpose, its collecting policy, and the clientele it is designed to serve will govern the kinds of records which are selected for preservation.

Records of agencies, organizations and institutions have administrative value. When working with such records, one must determine the office which has created the file, the extent of its authority, the research importance of the files, duplication of records in other files, and the location of the records. Records documenting policy formulation, data analysis, and constituency interaction are valuable. Convenient points of reference are the planning, organizing, staffing, directing, coordinating, reporting and budgeting functions. Records essential to the operation of an agency, business or institution and relating to its general management, personnel, responsibilities, legal rights, financial status and emergency situations are classed as vital. Financial and legal values may adhere to records and weigh in appraisal. Preservation of documents relating to financial authority, obligations and transactions which might be required for subsequent verification by audit must be considered; records used to prove the legal or civil rights of individuals to citizenship, property and employment must be preserved. The best-evidence rule requires the production of primary or original sources in court rather than secondary sources.

Research values which will allow for a new and better understanding of the human experience include those of uniqueness, credibility, understandability, time span and accessibility. The curator must determine if the information or the approach may be found in another published or unpublished source; if the authenticity and integrity of the document is intact; if the record is understandable and does not have meaning and value to the creator alone; whether there are enough samples over a period of time which will allow comparative analysis; and whether the information will be accessible, either physically or through arrangement.

Appraisal may, indeed, appear at times incongruous, inconsistent and contradictory. This situation may develop particularly when a curator of manuscripts appraises or assesses an archival record series. An archivist of public records may decide not to retain a series permanently; his decision may be governed by statute or administrative records retention policies. The record has no functional, evidential or informational value which mandates its permanent retention. However, a manuscript curator with knowledge of the lack of specific data, documentation, or resources (printed or unpublished) will deem the same series of permanent value. Two examples of experiences with such series at the University of Pittsburgh might be helpful in explication.

Inactive voters registration cards are not deemed by archivists to have permanent value and, therefore, are authorized for destruction. Street lists fall into the same category. However, if one is aware that there does not exist in Allegheny County a directory covering the county, the street lists are going to provide, at least to the extent that they do, a number of names of individuals in the county. Also, since the inactive voters registration records are arranged alphabetically while the street lists are arranged geographically, a mutual indexing system is established. One also considers other private manuscript groups which might be exploited by such discarded public record series. For example, in the Fulton Congressional Papers, held by the archives at the University of Pittsburgh, there is a series containing constituent questionnaires. These questionnaires, which requested an indication of opinion or attitude on major legislative issues, contain only the names and addresses of the individuals being polled; the inactive voters registration records will provide sociological data—race, residency, occupation, date of birth, place of birth, party affiliation—for the respondents to the questionnaires, if the respondents had registered to vote.

In addition to considering such potential informational and research value, processing, preservation and storage costs will be weighed against the prospective usefulness of the records acquired. It may be that there is a relatively small portion which should be retained.

The archivist then might select a portion that appears to constitute a representative part of the whole. Such samples can be statistical, functional, chronological, geographical or qualitative but must be done by experienced appraisal archivists in conjunction with administrators and researchers. The art of sampling is unrefined and there are no sure guidelines. Indeed, there is a real debate among archivists themselves as well as historians as to whether or not sampling should be adopted. Paul Lewinson's "Archival Sampling," published in *The American Archivist* (1957), deals in some detail with this problem.

Appraisal not only involves the record/manuscript group as a whole but is exercised at every level of arrangement. Weeding of units lacking continuing value may take place—routine acknowledgements, duplicates or extra letters, library and museum items. Care should be taken, however, before anything is permanently discarded; the items selected for removal might be held until the entire collection has been processed. Certainly this should be done when there is the least doubt as to its meaning or relationship to the entire collection.

While most concern in appraisal is that relating to permanent historical research and informational value, appraisal can include the setting of a monetary value. This is as difficult and uncertain, perhaps more so, as determining research value. Sale or tax appraisals should be based on fair market value and since so few manuscript collections or items, particularly of unheralded regional or local origin, are sold, it is difficult to set a monetary value based on market value. You may wish to consult the "Standards for Access and Appraisal of Gifts," endorsed by the SAA Executive Council in 1973 and published in the *American Archivist* (1974); "A Statement on Access to Original Research Materials in Libraries, Archives, and Manuscript Repositories," drafted by the Committee on Manuscript Collections of the Rare Books and Manuscripts Section of the Association of College and Research Libraries and approved in 1974, might be worth reading; this latter statement appeared in *College and Research Library News* (1974).

A list of appraisers (4th ed., August 1977) is available from the Society of American Archivists, Committee on Collecting Manuscripts, Manuscripts Department, University of Virginia Library, Charlottesville 22901. Send a stamped, self-addressed business-size envelope.

ARRANGEMENT

Arrangement is defined as

> the process and result of organizing archives, records, and manuscripts in accordance with accepted archival principles, particularly provenance, at as many as are necessary levels of the following levels: repository, record group or comparable unit, subgroup, series, file unit, and document. The process usually in-

cludes packing, labeling, and the shelving of archives, records and manuscripts and is intended to achieve physical or administrative control and basic identification of the holdings.

Arrangement is largely a process of grouping units in a meaningful inherent relationship to one another. By sorting and categorizing, an archivist/curator brings order and relationship, with the end being the revealing of the essential meaning and informational content of the records with which he works. The ready accessibility of the informational and evidential value of the record is what the curator/archivist attempts in arranging and describing historical materials.

The process of arrangement may begin before a body of records is transferred to the repository. One may conduct a preliminary survey to learn the nature and content of the material and secure during the organizing process an understanding of the collection's provenance, the history of the creating agency/institution/organization, biographical details of individuals, and information on specific functions or activities from which the record resulted. Indeed, the person responsible for the above may have overseen the methodical transfer of material to packing cartons and the labeling of those cartons with pertinent data.

Principles of Arrangement

Two principles, provenance and original order, the latter somewhat modifiable in application, have evolved as the major canons of archival theory from which archival procedures have derived. Until relatively recently, archives and manuscripts were considered so dissimilar that applying the same principles to both was considered impractical. However, the tremendous volume of nineteenth- and twentieth-century records and manuscripts has made these principles practically mandatory.

Provenance

In modern usage, the principle of provenance requires that records be maintained in the archives or manuscript repository according to the agency/office of creation — the office or administrative entity that created or received and accumulated the records in the conduct of its business. The agency of creation has been extended to include the person, family or other source of personal papers. In other words, there should be no intermingling of items from different manuscript groups. It is no longer acceptable, for example, to pull letters from/to a particular individual which may exist in three, four or whatever number of different manuscript groups and bring them together either in one original or artificial group for convenience, rapid access or whatever purpose.

Principle of Original Order

The second principle, that of maintaining records in the original order used by the office or agency that created them, is less rigid in application. Concern for original order in an archival record group should be exercised; however, with personal papers which may or may not systematically reflect the activity of its creator, the curator must be prepared to impose on a disarrayed collection an order based upon archival principles, manuscript techniques and research needs. A custodian of an archival record group which was created for its documentation or use may lean toward the "restoring" of original order, while a curator whose collections are primarily for research purposes might prefer imposing a new order or arrangement upon that which reveals little of the creator's personality or is difficult for researchers to use. In any event, archivists and curators will examine and analyze the record series carefully before either disrupting the original order in cases where such order exists, restoring original order where no apparent order is perceived, or modifying the order where there is a viable accessible order.

Levels of Arrangement

Arrangement takes place in various degrees on different levels: repository, record group/collection and subgroup, series, file unit, and document. Oliver W. Holmes describes this process in his article, "Archival Arrangement—Five Different Operations at Five Different Levels," which appeared in the *American Archivist* in 1964. A reading of that article will aid in clarifying what follows, since time and space permit only brief summarizations.

Record/Manuscript Group Level

A. Record Group. A record group is defined as a body of organizationally related records as established on the basis of provenance with particular regard for the administrative history, the complexity and the volume of the records and archives of the institution or organization involved. There are three kinds of record groups: 1) general groups which relate to an organization as a whole, not merely one unit of it; 2) record groups in which simply the records of the creating agency are kept together; 3) a collective group which brings bodies of records together—student publications.

B. Manuscript Group. A manuscript group is the counterpart of the record group in a manuscript repository. Manuscript groups have their origin in the non-government sector. This does not, however, mean that state archives or other public records archives do not contain such material. This can be readily seen by examining the *Guide to the Manuscript Groups in the Pennsylvania State Archives,* compiled by Harry E. Whipkey (1976). Manuscripts are: 1) bodies or groups of personal papers with organic unity; 2) an artificial collection of documents from various sources, usually according to a plan (autographs); 3) individual documents acquired by a repository because of their importance.

Series Level

The series is the most important level in arrangement because it is at this level that the archivist expresses the character of the group or collection by the divisions made of it:

A series is defined as

> file units or documents arranged in accordance with a filing system or maintained as a unit because they relate to a particular subject or function, result from the same activity, have a particular form, or because of some other relationship arising out of their creation, receipt, or use.

Processing cannot proceed without the series being determined and cannot be isolated before the archivist has studied the entire body of material.

Concern for original order first arises at the series level. The archivist/curator takes care that the disorder which may appear does not conceal a complicated, but precise, arrangement which might impinge/influence the accessibility to other series.

A series may be developed, created or arranged in accordance with chronology, topic, function of the creator, type of material. Archivists and curators tend to arrange series by function/activity or type. Arrangement by type segregates documents by their physical characteristics: minutes, financial documents, legal documents, scrapbooks. It is easy to recognize letterbooks, diaries, scrapbooks, deeds, etc., and, therefore, arrangement by type may prove easiest. Arrangement by subject is the most difficult because of the difficulty in determining the subject.

Series may be further divided into subseries. All series within a group/collection are arranged in order of the extent and value of the information within them.

File Unit Level

Within a series, there is the file unit. The file unit is an aggregate of documents brought together, usually for convenience of filing, in such a way that they may be treated as a unit: bound volumes, folders. File units may be arranged by type, chronology, alphabetically by topic, name, etc. Generally, the file unit is the lowest level at which an archivist works in larger repositories; frequently, the quantity and volume that are being processed in such repositories prevent detailed arrangement at the document level.

Document Level

Within a file unit, one finds documents. A document is a single record or manuscript item. When groups are small, arrangement will be done at this level—dating, cleaning, flattening. Arrangement may be chronological, alphabetical or a combination of both systems.

Repository Level

Collections may be arranged by chronological period, subject, etc. The arrangement at this level is purely for administrative control and is so accomplished to prevent costly shifting for collection expansion.

By the time all the processes of arrangement are completed, the curator/archivist will have gone through the collection several times: initial survey/acquisition, first sort, determination of series, final order.

SUMMARY

Appraisal and arrangement are two of the most crucial processes which an archivist or manuscript curator performs. While archival principles have evolved to the extent that they are generally applicable to private records as well as public records, the ultimate purpose of each repository, in part, will govern criteria used in appraisal and arrangement. While implementing methodology and procedures in order to conform to a standard, the archivist/curator must be open to novel conceptualization, procedural innovation and technical change to insure that what has been appraised merits permanent preservation and that its arrangement aids in utilization and exploitation by the researcher.

Description of Textual Records

By Frank M. Suran

THE work assignments of archivists and manuscript curators relate to three basic functions. These are to acquire, preserve and make available historically valuable records. Because of their importance, all of these functions deserve and require adequate expenditures of staff time and the allocation of other institutional resources. Records appraisal is a crucial first step because a hasty or careless decision could result either in the permanent loss of historical materials or in the commitment of time and money to records of marginal value. Those repositories that do not have conservation shops have found that even simple but necessary preservation procedures, such as unfolding, cleaning and flat-filing individual documents, are very time consuming. The final function of making records available to researchers involves the archival activities known as arrangement and description. The arrangement of records, the preparation of finding aids, and the responsibility for providing direct visitor and mail reference service to researchers also require a major commitment of staff. In coping with these numerous demands, the repository must strive to give proper attention to activities involving all three of its basic functions. This concern for balance is especially important when planning an effective descriptive program which will enable the repository to meet the needs of all researchers.

The purpose of this essay is to cover the basic elements of a descriptive program. These elements are discussed in much greater detail in David Gracy's *Archives and Manuscripts: Arrangement and Description,* Kenneth Duckett's *Modern Manuscripts: A Practical Manual for their Management, Care and Use,* T. R. Schellenberg's *The Management of Archives,* Lucille Kane's *A Guide to the Care and Administration of Manuscripts,* and *The Modern Manuscript Library* by Ruth Bordin and Robert Warner. The works by Duckett and Gracy should be found to be particularly useful. This essay draws most heavily from their works because of the clarity of their presentation and the comprehensive manner in which they deal with the description of records.

Before covering descriptive priorities for archival and manuscript repositories, it is necessary to define *description* and *finding aid.* Description is the process of establishing intellectual control over holdings through the preparation of finding aids. A finding aid is any descriptive medium, card or document, published or unpublished, that is created to establish physical or administrative and intellectual control over records. Finding aids have three primary objectives: 1) to provide information on all major collections in the repository; 2) provide information for particular types of researchers or specific subjects; 3) enable the repository staff to locate and retrieve the records. Thus, repositories must be concerned with finding aids relating to internal and external needs, ranging from a detailed published guide describing the holdings of the institution to a shelf list which notes the physical location of the records.

Three factors will have to be considered when determining the scope of a descriptive program. The first factor is the nature of the collections/record groups in the repository. Artificial collections and special collections of photographs, posters and similar material cannot be described as easily and effectively in a summary fashion as large series of records created to record the work of governmental or private agencies. The sheer quantity of records in a collection and the number of record and manuscript groups must be considered. Also, the relative significance of a collection or parts of a collection should be taken into account. All collections or segments of collections do not necessarily merit the same attention and concern for detail when being described.

The second factor is the reference needs of the repository. For example, government officials and historians usually require guides of a less precise nature than those needed by people engaged in purely genealogical research.

The third factor to consider in establishing a descriptive program is the size of the repository staff. If it is small, compromises will have to be made to achieve an effective and balanced descriptive program. Priorities will have to be set so certain finding aids can be prepared without undue attention being given to only a small portion of the holdings of the repository.

Once institutional priorities have been established, the archivist/manuscript curator can begin work on a descriptive program utilizing the following types of finding aids:

1. *Accession Register*
The accession register is used to establish initial physical, legal and intellectual control over new holdings. The register should contain:
1) an accession number which can be used to identify the records
2) the date the records were received
3) the donor's name and address
4) the type of accession — transfer of records, gift, loan or purchase
5) a brief description of the accession emphasizing the record types, appropriate dates, prominent subjects or individuals. If during the course of the initial inspection, information on the new accession

comes easily, the descriptive statement should be expanded. This should prove useful if the collection will not be processed for a long period of time.

Accession Register Descriptive Entries

> Description: Account books and general correspondence (inc. bills, invoices, advertisements, etc.) of W. L. Barclay and his sons S. D. and George S. Barclay pertaining to family business and financial interests, ca. 1906-1934. Records relate in large part to the Barclay Chemical Company (Lacquin plant and the home offices at Williamsport), Lacquin Lumber Co., and the Northwest Lumber Co. (Seattle, Wash.). 8 cubic feet.

> Description: Records of the Office of the Prothonotary, Huntingdon County: medical register, 1881-1945; appearance dockets, 1797-1856 (9 vols.); register of motor vehicles, 1903; and Common Pleas minute books, 1802-1905 (10 vols.). 6 cubic feet.

6) the temporary location of the new accession and, if determined, the name of the record or manuscript group to which it will be assigned.

The accessions register is an extremely useful descriptive tool as it:
1) provides inventory control before the collection is fully arranged and described; 2) can be used as a temporary finding aid; 3) can be used to prepare donor, agency and even subject/correspondent indices; 4) provides a preliminary analysis of a collection which can be utilized in preparing the National Union Catalog of Manuscript Collections Data Sheet.

NUCMC Catalog Card as prepared from Data Sheet Description
(compare to similar example under Accession Register Entries)

MS 76-659

> *Barclay family*
> Papers, 1906-34.   8 ft.
> In Pennsylvania Historical and Museum Commission collections (Harrisburg)
> Correspondence, account books, bills, and invoices, relating to the family's business and financial interests, particularly Barclay Chemical Company, Williamsport, Pa., its plant at Lacquin, Pa., Lacquin Lumber Company, and Northwest Lumber Company, Seattle, Wash. Persons represented include W. L. Barclay and his sons, George S. and S. D. Barclay.
> Unpublished finding aid in the repository.
> Permanent deposit by Mrs. Stanley Barclay, Jersey Shore, PA., 1973.

2. *Inventory*

The inventory is particularly useful in describing large collections or record groups. Depending on the depth of the arrangement of the collection/record group and whether it is considered significant enough for publication, it could consist of seven sections. The sections of the inventory are: 1) introduction; 2) biographical-agency sketch; 3) scope and content note; 4) series description; 5) container/box list; 6) item list and index; 7) preface.

Sections two through five appear in most inventories. The biographical agency sketch should provide the researcher with information regarding the administrative history of the agency whose records are being described, or if it is the papers of an individual, an account of his life and accomplishments. The scope and content note provides general information about the types of records in the manuscript/record group, the period covered, and subjects and individuals most prominently mentioned.

Scope and Content note — Guide entry for Manuscript Group

> MG—237 SECOND TROOP, PHILADELPHIA CITY CAVALRY COLLECTION, 1810-1941.   1 cu. ft.
>
> Records of or pertaining to the Second Troop, Philadelphia City Cavalry, a military company first organized during the Revolution at the direction of the Committee of Correspondence of Philadelphia City and County. After being disbanded in 1850, the troop was reorganized in 1896.
>
> Correspondence, 1821-22 (copies), 1902, 1909-13, 5 folders, relates almost exclusively to the work of the 2nd Troop Association's Committee on Troop History, chaired by Dr. W. A. Newman Dorland, which was assigned the task of gathering material for a history of the organization. Prominent correspondents include Herman V. Ames, John W. Jordan, Luther R. Kelker, Thomas L. Montgomery, Thomas J. Stewart, and Irving C. Wilson.
>
> Troop records include minutes, 1898; a report of the troop's commanding officer, 1901; memorandums and various membership, enlistment, and mailing lists, 1908-14; by-laws, 1810, 1915; 3 folders of photographs of military camp scenes apparently taken in 1926; 2 scrapbooks, 1896-1902; and miscellaneous papers and accounts, 1900-41. Collection also includes an early photographic copy of a letter from Abraham Lincoln to General U. S. Grant, dated April 14, 1865.

Each series is described individually. The description usually notes the physical type or types (letters, reports, diaries, ledgers, etc.) of records making up the series, inclusive dates, standard information contained in certain record types, and principal correspondents and topics.

Series Description

> CLEMENCY FILE. 1874-1900, 1906-1907. 70 cu. ft.
>
> Arranged alphabetically by name of petitioner for clemency.
>
> Individual case files considered by the Board of Pardons, usually consisting of a summary sheet of all official actions, letters and petitions supporting and opposing the appeal, court

transcripts, newspaper notices, and copies of death warrants, pardon proclamations, respites, and related documents. The file includes the appeals of Alexander Berkman, several reputed "Molly Maguires," and other individuals involved in labor disturbances.

REGISTER OF MINE ACCIDENTS. 1899-1972. 38 VOLS. 19.4 cu. ft.

Arranged by coal mining districts and thereafter chronologically.

A record of mining accidents in the bituminous and anthracite coal districts. Entries show the mining district and its inspector's name, the date of the accident, the name of the mine, the specific causes of the mishap, the number of persons injured, and whether the injuries proved fatal. Information listed about the miners includes their names, age, nationality, marital status, number of children, citizen or alien, and their job in the mine.

The container list enables the researcher and the staff to quickly scan record series and locate appropriate materials. It gives a folder-by-folder description of the contents of each box in the collection/record group.

Box listing for Correspondence Series

	Folders	Box
Juniata College, 1904 (M. G. Brumbaugh)	1	35
Ke-Ku, 1903-06	1	
Keen, Gregory B., 1903-07 (Sec. — Historical Soc. of Penna.)	1	
Knox, P. C., 1905-06	1	
Kriebel, Rev. O. S., 1904-06 (Perkiomen Seminary)	1	
La-Li, 1903-06	1	
Lamberton, James M., 1903-07 (Corresponding Secy. —Historical Soc. of Dauphin Co.)	1	
Landis, John H., 1903-06	1	

3. *General Card Catalog*

The general card catalog is the most efficient in-house finding aid. Cards for correspondents, subjects, and important individuals mentioned in the records should be maintained in the repository reading room. The cards can be made from information contained in the accession-register description, appropriate sections of the inventory, or another perusal of the records. The size of the repository's staff will determine the amount of indexing it will be able to do. The cards can be quite simple, merely listing a record/manuscript group number or numbers under the heading. Also, if resources are limited, it is important to be selective in the preparation of the cards.

Each individual collection/record group should also be maintained in a main card file. These cards would give the same type of descriptive information contained on the NUCMC catalog card. This control system will enable a researcher to go from a subject card, to a brief description of the collection in the main card file, to an inventory which may contain a box and item listing relating to the series in question.

4. *Information Brochures and Leaflets*

Brief information bulletins are easy to prepare, relatively inexpensive to print, and relieve the staff in answering standard inquiries on the holdings and services of the repository. The Information Leaflets of the National Archives are good examples of this finding aid.

5. *Journals and Subject Guide Projects*

All collections eligible for inclusion in the National Union Catalog of Manuscript Collections, published by the Library of Congress, should be reported. The repository should also cooperate with editors preparing subject guides relating to the holdings of many institutions. Also, many historical and professional journals will print information on new accessions and records openings in their news notes sections. Repositories should take advantage of these published finding aids because they reach a large audience and require only a temporary commitment of staff time to prepare the necessary reporting forms.

6. *Guides*

At the repository level, a guide is a finding aid (usually published) that describes the holdings of a repository, with record groups and manuscript groups serving as the main units of entry. For archival records, it could be a summary guide that lists only the series within each record group, or a detailed guide that includes detailed descriptions of each series. Manuscript collections are usually described in the same format used in the inventory scope and content note.

SUMMARY

The maintenance of an accession register or file and a modest card catalog, the preparation of inventories for major collections/record groups, contributions to special subject guides and to external publications such as those sponsored by the National Historical Publications and Records Commission and the Library of Congress, and the publication of appropriate information leaflets and a general guide to the holdings of the repository are the major components of a balanced and comprehensive descriptive program. The preparation of these finding aids should enable the staff of the repository to more easily handle the entire range of reference demands, and at the same time allow the archivists/manuscript curators to attend to other archival activities.

Non-Textual Records (Photographs)

By Elisabeth W. Betz

PICTURES are generally found in the holdings of most archival agencies and libraries. Such non-textual records, because of physical and research problems, need to be stored and accessed in a different way from textual records. Photographs usually form the bulk of these pictorial records.

In regard to physical problems, one must be aware that photographs are especially elusive because of the processes by which they are made. Chemical reactions may take place within a photo or negative over a period of time, and they will deteriorate if proper care is not provided. Other papers in the same file may chemically contaminate the photographic emulsion. Physical damage may also occur in use; without enough support the photos or prints will curl, fold or tear when material is removed from or put into the file, and very large or very small pictures are likely to be torn or marred by fingerprints when handled.

Research with pictorial materials is of growing interest. Prints and photographs can be used — with appropriate caution — as primary sources. Diaries, letters and indeed all manuscripts, as well as public documents, such as census and immigration records, are being examined by the modern researcher to discover the past in contemporary terms. *Pictures* help us to reconstruct — in a more immediate way than texts can — physical changes in landscape and life. In contrast to images, textual records contain internal evidence as to the contents and hence a vocabulary with which to describe them. Pictorial material is often not self-explanatory and, therefore, requires more effort in organization and cataloging for access.

Pictorial materials, especially photographs, often have little or no identification because at the time the images were made or collected, the facts about them were known and therefore not recorded. Do not remove any images from textual records without first transferring vital information — in pencil — onto the back of each piece or on a coordinated list. Also, exercise caution in accepting the complete accuracy of a caption. People expect photographs at least to be truthful, but one must be wary of identifications that are attached to all visual material. Collectors and creators of visual records may interpret the truth to fit their needs or not have sufficient information to confirm their identification. (News service photo captions are notorious for inaccuracies, as are nineteenth-century historical prints.)

A general knowledge of the history of photography provides a basis for determining what it was technically possible to record at a particular time and what the physical problems were. For example, except during the earliest period, stereos were curved: they can be dated generally by this physical characteristic as well as by the various color-coded mounts. Curved stereos should, of course, not be flattened. Books listed in the bibliography of this paper give detailed descriptions of various types of photographs, such as daguerreotypes, tintypes, gold-toned albumen prints and *cartes-de-visite*. For the most part, the date, photographer, image information and the iconography are probably more important facts to identify than the photographic process. However, the photographic process or the type of photo (such as *carte-de-visite*) can give clues to the actual date or period of the photo.

Newsprint, which is filled with destructive acid, and photocopies on inferior paper should not remain in the same envelopes as prints and photos. If an image exists only in a negative form, the caption should either be copied onto the negative jacket in pencil or photocopied on high-quality paper and inserted into the jacket on the non-emulsion side of the negative. Sometimes it is impossible to use a negative collection without first transferring the negative and caption information from disintegrating Kraft-paper envelopes.

After all the identification has been recorded, each item should be protected. Cellulose triacetate or polyester transparent sleeves for each piece within a box are suggested. Paper jackets may absorb moisture, which results in chemical reactions and mold growth. Although the polyester sleeves may be best for archival storage, acid-free buffered envelopes are less expensive and will certainly work satisfactorily if the atmospheric conditions are watched. (Other approved containers and materials for archival preservation are available.) The cardinal rule is to maintain a consistently cold and dry atmosphere: the temperature should be no more than seventy degrees and the humidity no more than forty per cent.

Instead of using individual sleeves, you can also store a group of unmounted photos in an envelope that is supported with acid-free, buffered board as a means of reducing mechanical wear and tear. Glacine envelopes are definitely inadvisable. Scotch tape should be removed if it comes off easily; rubber bands, paper clips and other metal fasteners that rust should be discarded.

Interleave high-quality paper or sheets of transparent polyester film (often called Mylar) between the pages of albums to keep images from leaching through the opposite page. It is possible to do Mylar encapsulation of

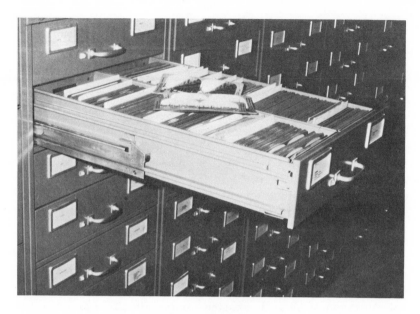

Stereograph file

Acidic negative jackets with caption information

individual items yourself: Mylar, an alignment device, and double-stick tape are sold by the Hollinger Corporation and others. Mylar encapsulation is the best kind of protection available for prints that are fragile, large, apt to tear, damaged already, or handled frequently. Copy photos of the objects can be made through the Mylar cover. It is wasted effort to encapsulate large numbers of photographs — individual transparent sleeves that are open on one or two sides or paper envelopes are more practical protectors.

After the prints and photos have been properly protected, they should be put into boxes according to size and number. Smaller items can be stored upright in document boxes and larger pieces in flat horizontal boxes, and oversize material can be filed in baked-on-enamel metal map cases.

As you proceed in boxing the photos and prints, original and copy negatives should be coordinated with a coding system. If the pictorial material is closely related or an integral part of text, the curator should be sure to record that fact on both pieces.

Negatives should be filed separately from prints, partly for efficiency, but also because they require a more stringently controlled climate. Negatives must be stored in acid-free, buffered paper jackets in baked-on-enamel metal filing cabinets. They should only be handled with lint-free cloth gloves (available at camera shops) so that fingerprints do not permanently obscure the images. Glass-plate negatives should be put into smaller boxes or between dividers within the drawers so that the motion of opening and closing does not crack or break the negatives.

Segregate nitrate film from safety film. After 1950 the words "Safety film" are printed on the edge; pre-1950 film may have to be tested, but in general nitrate film is identifiable by its muddy brown color and a peculiar smell. Nitrate film damages material with which it is in close contact and is very volatile when enclosed in containers without circulating air. All negatives should be stored in individual jackets in a cool room with ventilation; the colder the temperature the longer the lifespan of the negatives. Although small numbers of nitrate negatives can be stored for some time under the conditions just described, they should be converted to safety film. Nitrate negatives can still be used to make prints.

As pictorial material is copied for researchers, the copy negatives should be filed in their own sequential number system, with the negative number recorded on the original. Of course, this system can be applied to non-pictorial material also and the copy negatives interfiled.

Conservation is a new field. This is especially true of photographic conservation because so few people have had adequate practical experience. One should not undertake elaborate repairs without proper supervision by

Boxes and map case for storage of pictorial material of different sizes

*Glass-plate negative storage in baked-on-enamel filing cabinets
with drawer dividers*

a trained conservator. Sometimes it may be just as well to handle the material as carefully as possible or to supply substitutes for researchers in the form of record photographs, microfilm or microfiche. (Textual records pose similar problems.) Images with stains can be photographically copied with filters.

If you want to mount images on cardboard, do so only with non-critical material or copies and use acid-free, buffered board. Do no apply rubber cement or sticky tape. One might consider polyvinyl glue. Before dry-mounting or any kind of mounting, all the information on the back of the print or photo should be recorded on a caption card or strip no matter how irrelevant it seems because it may later prove to be the missing link to complete identification of the image.

It is extremely difficult to reverse the process of mounting. Prints that have been glued or taped onto mounts eventually show the effects of staining. Older mounts are no doubt acidic and therefore brittle. Even if the image is stable, the mount may crack underneath. Never attempt to soak photos off mounts. An acidic mount may be better left as is, unless the image is being damaged.

Curled and folded brittle prints and photographs should not be opened. Items that are stuck together should not be forced apart. Sometimes such material, when left in a dry, cold place, will "relax" and straighten out or come apart naturally. Prints and photos that are framed should be removed, as it is likely the framing materials are acidic and the image moldy. If a photograph is framed without a mat, the emulsion may be sticking to the glass because of condensation. A daguerreotype, on the other hand, is sandwiched between glass, often with an elaborate outside case. Precluding a growing deterioration inside, it should be left in the case, which has a historical value in its own right.

There are two basic means of providing access to pictorial materials. One is to preserve a record group of prints and photos or to form a new group (an artificial collection) of items which, although they may have been acquired separately, logically belong together. The other is to integrate single items into various self-indexing vertical files.

Single prints and photographs can be put into envelopes supported by acid-free, buffered boards and filed vertically into standard metal cabinets. (One is, of course, limited to material that fits within the dimensions of the file drawer.) They can also be dry-mounted with the caption information typed onto strips of acid-free paper and affixed to the top front side of the mount; then a researcher can identify a particular image quickly without having to pull it entirely out of the drawer. The arrangement of the material can be indicated by large guide cards within the files, thus eliminating the need for an exterior index. Basic files are biographical,

Brittle, acidic mounting board

Mounted copy photograph with caption strip

geographical and subject. Be sure the filing location is written on each piece, and a listing of all the headings and cross-references is maintained to keep consistent terminology, spelling and logic throughout a particular file.

Group collections that belong with textual material should be shelved in close proximity, probably in the last containers of the record group. If the group consists entirely of visual records, it should be assigned a shelf location. As with the material in self-indexing files, each item should be marked in pencil with the location designation so that anything removed can be returned to its proper place.

All non-textual records require identification and arrangement. Most groups do not need complete cataloging of each item. The scope, size and uniqueness of the collection determine the depth to which inventorying and cataloging should be done. The clientele to be served is also a factor. Pictorial material that has been culled from textual records will be organized basically according to the original order of those records; coordination is very important here. A collection consisting of pictures can be dealt with in much the same fashion as archival textual records in which the original order is preserved. Pictorial collections arriving in disarray, however, must be given a structure. By examining each collection as a whole, an arrangement can be selected that is best suited for access: by subject, by date, by photographer or artist, by medium or by location—or a combination of these categories.

Further intellectual access can be gained through the traditional finding aids used in archives. However, the larger the collection the greater the need (and our responsibility) for detailed, *analytical* documentation. The historical or informational value of the material, as well as its value as artifacts, are points to be considered in the amount of documentation that is done. Pictorial research is approached differently from written records or printed books. *Verbal*, interpretive access must be provided in any case. Portraits and biographical material, geographical places, historical events, concepts, subjects and illustrations of hard-to-find objects should be indexed in order to help researchers.

A manual system of retrieval is accomplished most efficiently by cards. A card file is easy to update and is a method for integrating information from various sources in one place. Typing one card for each entry that you want to make is extremely tedious; the best solution is to find a means of getting multiple copies of the cards by a photocopying process or through the use of a word-processing machine. As with files, the most basic indexes you should have are biographical, geographical, subject and chronological. It is imperative to keep track of the subjects and name headings you use so that the same terms are consistently applied. A sufficient number of subject and name entries in the card indexes helps the researcher to assess the usefulness of the materials before calling for their retrieval, thus protecting the collections from unnecessary exposure and handling. The success of the indexes depends on careful analysis of the images and calculation of future reference needs. If it is not possible to have cards made in multiple copies, then a heading that refers the user to the location of the original item is helpful. Several access points can be tagged for each image or collection and reference cards made. There should be one card with the complete caption.

Storage and control of non-textual records is problematic. When they are mixed with textual materials or are varying media themselves, far greater complications arise. By using a combination of museum techniques of control, archival and manuscript control, and emphasizing subject analysis, as done in libraries, we can offer the modern researcher extensive access.

Cartographic Records

By Leon J. Stout

CURATORS and archivists in charge of small historical repositories often face the challenge of dealing with those ungainly and awkward creatures known as maps. They are usually found rolled up and standing in a corner or buried in a map case, sharing oversize storage with posters, prints and other large-format materials. Or a map may be suddenly rediscovered when you hear a patron ask, "Exactly where was that old railroad's Reno station?" It is rather unlikely that archivists/curators will have to deal with maps as cartographic archives since only the largest archival units serve organizations or government agencies with major map production responsibilities. Most small historical agencies will perform a curatorial function in relation to their maps and related cartographic materials. Nevertheless, college archives and repositories holding some types of business and local government records may have maps or measured drawings which require an archival approach. For this reason, the archival and the curatorial approaches will be compared and a middle path illustrated for those repositories which cannot support either full library-style cataloging or a complete archival processing procedure.

It is common to think of a map essentially as an aid to travel, but this is only one way in which a map is used. General historical maps portray areas of concern in many patterns, each contributing to historical understanding. They may help in locating demolished structures or early transportation routes, or in etermining the density of ethic settlement. Old maps can help engineers locate old springs or stream beds that affect new construction. They can tell genealogists where ancestors lived or where they owned land. Furthermore, maps are excellent for illustrating and dramatizing historical publications and exhibits. The list of uses is large.

What exactly are these sheets which so graphically provide such information? A map, according to one author, is an "abstract, abbreviated representation of a part or a whole of an area, usually the earth's surface." One should be aware that maps are categorized in many ways. Basically these are:

1) general—such as the National Geographic Society map of the United States;

2) special purpose—for example, a State Department of Transportation road map of Pennsylvania; and

3) thematic—the one-factor map, such as a township land-use map.

The small repository probably has examples of all three categories, although it is likely to have additional types such as:

4) manuscript—hand-drawn sketch maps, say of a neighborhood, or a land survey to scale;

5) aerial—photomosaics perhaps, taken from airplanes, and now also from satellites; and

6) architectural or engineering drawings—such as the blueprints of the local gristmill recently added to the National Register.

From the archival standpoint, the above types can also be described as cartographic records. As "cartographic" they are maps, and as "records" they would be the non-current records of an organization preserved for legal, administrative or historical purposes. These maps would be either those produced as a main function of an agency or those collected by that agency in its day-to-day activities. There might also be "related records," such as survey notes and other papers relating to the production of maps themselves. Small repositories and college archives holding cartographic records would be wise to adopt the *basic* framework of the archival approach outlined below when dealing with such records.

FIVE BASIC ELEMENTS OF MANAGEMENT

1. *Accessions and Acquisitions*

Ignoring for the moment those maps already hidden away in a repository closet, where do maps come from? In a cartographic archives, maps will "arrive." While some may show up virtually unheralded, most accessions require some initiative on the part of the archivist in surveying the extant cartographic records and developing a schedule for the office of origin to follow in transferring maps to the archives. For example, a college archive should indicate the need for the transfer of plans of demolished buildings or property inventory maps as they become inactive or outdated. Initiative frequently means reminding agencies when it's time to transfer records.

In contrast to the archivist, the map librarian or cartographic curator will have two basic approaches. He can simply sit and wait for maps to arrive as gifts—some always do. However, the more resourceful approach is to seek them out for purchase or donation. Historical maps may be acquired through dealers, such as Argosy Book Store and The Cartographer in New York.* Other sources for historical maps and atlases of local inter-

---

*See bibliography for list of dealers

est are estate auctions and local antique dealers. Reproduction dealers, such as Historic Urban Plans, or even photocopies from the Library of Congress or the National Archives may also be sources. In acquiring originals, however, one should be prepared for the rude shock of learning that many of these maps are quite expensive, with prices in the hundreds of dollars not uncommon.

There is another tack that can be taken. You should think to the future and acquire maps of local interest being produced today. Fortunately, many of these are government-produced and are either free or inexpensive. In Pennsylvania, the Departments of Commerce and Transportation, the Bureau of Aviation, the Topographic and Geological Survey, and the Bureau of Land Records all produce maps. The federal government obviously should not be overlooked and lists of agencies that produce maps are readily available.* In traveling this route one should also consider maps from county and municipal agencies, such as planning or zoning boards, or from public utilities — over the years these will become historical sources as well.

2. *Arrangement and Classification*

The maps have arrived and this fact has been recorded in your accessions record. How should the maps be arranged for easiest access? In an archival setting you will be following the standard method of control by provenance — that is the maps will be assigned to a record group by their office of origin. You then arrange them into series by function or activity represented, say, campus building plans in one series, landscaping in another. If they seem to be more an agglomeration of maps, perhaps a "general cartographic records" series will suffice. The object here is hierarchical control and the removal of cartographic records from those of other formats into separate series. Arrangement within a series will typically be by the existing numerical system if the maps form some type of set. If the maps are more a miscellany, they should be arranged chronologically by area. Another concern in the archival approach is the need to file the maps together as a group, ideally in a block of map-case drawers.

The archival approach, as explained above, stresses the interrelationships of the maps because of their similar origin or their similar use by an agency. On the other hand, the curatorial approach asserts the independence of each map as a discrete entity. In arrangement, a concession is made to the user by trying to group maps of like areas together. The classification system is a detailed, logical method of doing this and a system which is infinitely expandable. One of the most popular is the Library of Congress classification system's G-schedule. For example under this sys-

---

*See bibliography for lists of agencies

tem, a map of State College, Pennsylvania, produced by the Centre County Planning Commission in 1960, would receive the following number:

G3824 for Pennsylvania city and town maps

.S7 for State College (a "Cutter" number)

1960 the date of the map

.C4 the authority (another "Cutter" number)

Since a classification system is essentially a filing system, you can see that all maps of State College, regardless of date or author, would be filed together. This is an expensive process as the size of the collection grows, since you must keep track of all previous maps classified to avoid duplicating a number.

There are alternatives. In one situation, if a donor presents a collection of maps—the John Doe Coal Mine Maps, for example—there is no reason why this collection should not be kept intact, and added to when possible. But, if the collection is small and general (less than two or three hundred maps), a quicker system might be filing maps in drawers by area, and numbering each drawer and each map in each drawer. Thus in the handlist or card catalog, maps would simply be referenced by the numbers, "2-8" for example (i.e., the eighth map in the second drawer). This should not be used in a collection where extensive growth is expected, since there will be much reshuffling of maps and relabelling of folders, cards, lists, etc.

3. *Description and Cataloging*

Now that you have determined how your maps will be arranged, you must consider how to gain access to them. In small collections with sufficient labelling of drawers, folders, etc., the filing system might be self-indexing, and there would be no surrogate list, inventory or card catalog. However, when memory fails, every request means a trip to the map files, and an actual search through the materials to see if you have such a map. This is inefficient and may lead to physical deterioration of the maps. The purpose of a finding aid is to enable you to make a reasonable judgment as to whether or not any of your maps can answer a particular question without you actually looking at them. Again, the question becomes—do you work with aggregates of material or single items?

The archival approach assumes that aggregate description is sufficient because of the similarities of the material and the cost inefficiency of single-item cataloging. Here the series description is the primary finding aid. In general it will tell you: the inclusive dates of the material, the number of items, the reason for their creation, the types of information they include, and the topics or areas covered. In some general cartographic record series, the series description may end up being a brief item list. The user may also be aided by the existence of the creating agency's item-based finding aid (card file, list or index maps). Finally in some archival situations, extra help may permit the creation of an item-based finding aid within the repository. The National Archives new experimental card system, designed by William J. Heynen, is shown in the accompanying figure. It is being used for single items or small groups of like items.

RECORD GROUP	220-Presidential Committees National Resources Cte.
SERIES	Drainage Basin Subdivisions
FILE UNIT	19-5

Map of Northwestern Pennsylvania showing the outlines of the summit water basins.

DATE	1900	NO. OF ITEMS	1
PHYSICAL TYPE	Litho.
SCALE	1 inch=7.8 miles
SIZE	22" x 16.5"

MAP CATALOG

NOTE: an *invented* addition to a NARS series.

GSA FORM **7220** (3-76)

In the curatorial approach to single-item cataloging, the assumption is made that each item is worth a relatively equal investment in terms of description. Unfortunately, this may not always be true. The arguments in the field of map cataloging have not been concerned with this matter, but rather with the selection of data elements and their placement on the catalog card. Basically, there are two camps. Those who seek conformity with general library cataloging will use the Anglo-American Cataloging Rules (AACR) and head their cards with the creating authority, usually the cartographer or publisher. Those who feel this to be unnecessary and irrelevant to the user will use some type of area descriptor, date, scale and map type. The AACR proponents will note that this type of information can be had through subject headings on additional cards; however, most map curators' experience indicates that a user's approach by cartographer or publisher is rare.

If your central finding aid or card catalog has an established system for preparing cards, it would probably be wise to follow it. If not, a card file with area headings will probably prove most useful. If the map collection is small, perhaps supplementary lists or photocopies of catalog cards could be used to index map authors, subjects (e.g., agriculture, transportation, etc.), or other special features.

Automation is one further consideration for the future. If may seem utopian to many of us, but in some libraries maps are being included in computer data bases, such as the Ohio College Libraries Center's (OCLC) and LC's Machine Readable Cataloging—Maps (MARC-MAPS). If you are in a library with access to OCLC, perhaps you will want to consider investing in formal cataloging to place your maps in this national data base. A side benefit to formal description is the ability to respond to calls for union listings of maps, a tool which will become ever more necessary to researchers in the future.

4. *Storage and Preservation*

Regardless of whether you have archival or curatorial responsibilities, the needs here are the same. The proper environments of repositories and an in-depth treatment of preservation and repair of materials is the province of other authors in this manual. Nevertheless, there are some special considerations that you should be aware of in dealing with maps. In the area of storage, flat-map cases—sometimes known as blueprint cases— are virtually the standard method. The object, whether you use flat or vertical cases, is to keep the maps *flat* (not folded). Naturally, not everything will fit your map cases, so you might compromise by either rolling oversize maps and storing them in tubes or dissecting them into parts that will fit the case. Or, like the National Archives, you might purchase a stand of seventy-five-inch-wide map cases. The drawers should be no more than two inches deep to avoid tears when removing and replacing maps and to make identification easier. The drawers should have dust covers which prevent the buckling of maps at the back when closing the drawer. For maps that should be kept from further deterioration, acid-free map folders should be used.

Reinforcement is another area of concern with maps. Mylar encapsulation (discussed elsewhere) is now the preferred method of strengthening maps. Silking and canvas-backing are futile, since the paper frequently outlasts the backing. Lamination has been given up by both the Library of Congress and the National Archives' Center for Cartographic and Architectural Archives. The latter process darkens paper, causes some inks to run, and cannot be undone with any predictable degree of safety for the map. Lamination should be considered only for maps that can be easily replaced or have no continuing research or monetary value. Mylar encapsulation should ideally be preceded by deacidification. Lamination without deacidification will not halt further deterioration from the effects of acid. One further point of interest here is that LC's Geography and Maps

Division is now disbinding their county atlases, deacidifying the maps, encapsulating them and mounting them in post binders for reference use.

The microfilming of maps is one final possibility, which for most repositories is not feasible at this time. It was long known that 35 mm. and 16 mm. microfilm was virtually useless for maps. However, work at the National Archives, Public Archives of Canada, and other like centers has indicated that the filming of maps on 105 mm. stock can be quite acceptable. The National Archives has filmed as a pilot project approximately twelve hundred early General Land Office maps in color and black and white on film chips about the size of microfiche. They are exceptionally clear and could prove a future boon to research libraries and archives.

5. *Reference Services*

Beyond efficient arrangement and description of maps in good condition, what should the repository provide for the user? Common sence suggests a large table or two and perhaps a tracing table and photocopy service for same-size copies or image reduction. A repository might also consider a reasonably good set of cartographic reference books,* or at least appropriate general, historical and topical atlases. The holdings lists, accession lists and guides to maps and map collections in your state would also be of significant help in reference service. If your area is not well-covered by a gazetteer or by an up-to-date place-names reference, you might consider producing or having a volunteer do a local place-names booklet to aid in map reference.

Beyond these amenities to researchers, the archivist or curator should be aware of the impact of the new copyright law on photocopying of his materials. When providing photocopying service, one should also be concerned for the physical condition of older maps and atlases in particular — err on the side of preservation rather than please the user when you have doubts here.

What type of users might one expect for maps? What collateral materials might you consider acquiring? Of course, this will vary depending on the type of institution. However, in any local historical repository, genealogy will probably be a major use (at the National Archives Center for Cartographic and Architectural Archives almost forty per cent of their "walk-in trade" is genealogists). Here any maps which can link people to specific places will be of use. County warrantee maps, Sanborn atlases, nineteenth-century county atlases, and wall maps are useful, as are old survey maps, plat books, and of collateral use, copies of the indexes compiled for the state (and perhaps neighboring states) federal census schedules.

---

*See bibliography for articles giving information

Archival and curatorial approaches to maps have been compared throughout this paper. Is there a similar difference in reference work or in the approach of the user? In general we can say that cartographic archives users will find their answers by pursuing the records of an agency that affected the area or subject they're interested in. For example, a historian interested in the Centennial Exhibition of 1876 would check the Philadelphia City and County Archives, where he can use Record Group 231, Series 7, Papers of the Architect and Engineer's Office, to consult maps and surveys of the exhibition grounds. The same user of a map collection organized on library principles would go to the card catalog and look up, say, PHILADELPHIA. CENTENNIAL EXHIBITION 1876, and hope he might find maps.

This does impose a greater burden on the archivist for he must be more conversant with both his collections and the activities of the agencies whose records he holds. The curator may be aware of good maps on a particular subject, but he is spared using the search strategy which employs determining what agency did what, when and where before one hazards a look at a finding aid to see if the agency produced or used any maps in that work.

CONCLUSION

In any event, maps, due to their physical format, are frequently neglected in the day-to-day work of helping researchers. This obviously should not be. They are great treasures—textual and graphic at the same time. Their use is growing and they are finally receiving their due from researchers and keepers of historical materials alike. Bring your maps out of the closet, acquire new ones, arrange them, describe them, share information about them with other repositories, and utilize them in responding to researchers; they are worth the extra effort.

Part 3

PLANNING FOR USERS, SECURITY AND SPACE

Reference

By George Chalou

ARCHIVISTS, manuscript curators, and librarians share something very important. In truth, what they share reaches to the very heart of why historical societies through the years have collected and organized records. Through record keeping, persons, institutions and governments have the means of retrieving the essence of their past activities. Those who provide reference service are engaged in making records, historical manuscripts and books available. This means constant interaction with the user of the documentary resources in our custody. Because reference service is an action function and because reference work is never quite done, seldom is there an opportunity for a reference staff to reflect on the nature of reference service.

If one could peer through the roof and ceiling of an institution, this typical and dynamic scene might be viewed. He might see large financial account books being loaded on a record cart to be delivered shortly to a user in the reference room. There one might see a researcher and a staff person in animated conversation. Facial expressions and body language indicate that this is where the action is taking place. The records, the staff member, and the researcher have come together. The viewer might just have witnessed what could be termed the point of convergence.

All three of these necessary elements of reference service — records, staff and users — must be properly prepared and combined for maximum benefit. Because reference service takes so much of a staff's time, little thought is given to the analysis of this service. Yet careful study and attention must be given if institutions desire to continue providing high-quality reference service. The first element, the records, is inanimate and, of course, reflects what the creators, transmitters and recipients of the records have done with them. Records that are created on a stable physical base and are properly maintained will be in better condition for users. Proper preservation of records and historical manuscripts must take precedence over the needs of researchers. Making a fragile document available to one person could destroy the document forever, or more probably, could mean an expensive repair for an organization. Records also must be boxed, labeled and arranged in order to help your users and your staff. In addition, the more finding aids, such as inventories, calendars, indexes and guides, an organization prepares the more efficient the reference operation.

The reference staff should hold positive attitudes toward people and provide a service to researchers. This underlying attitude is very important and should be demonstrated throughout the organization. However, wanting to help a researcher is sometimes not enough if the organization does not have adequate reference staff. Administrators should study the past reference load in order to prepare for heavy-use periods. College vacations or holiday breaks usually bring more users into a library or historical society facility. Most organizations have back-up personnel who can be called upon for temporary duty during unexpectedly heavy researcher use.

The users of a particular institution's holdings may represent a cross section of the research community or a specialized clientele. Many factors affect this composition, but the subject matter of the records is the most significant. The particular location of the library or archives and the quality of service researchers can expect are also important. An institution has control over the quality of records and staff, but possesses little control over the quality of researchers. Those persons, however, who read the secondary literature on their topic and carefully design their research before using records will be easier to work with and will profit more from a visit to a research facility.

Well-prepared users, a motivated and trained reference staff, and properly maintained records come together in such a way that all three benefit. If one element is weak, then less than full utilization of the records will occur. If the staff is inadequate and the user unprepared, the most carefully maintained and fully described records will be underused. It is important that every repository do all that it can to develop all three elements — records, staff and users.

In addition to understanding the nature of reference, it is important to distinguish the various forms of reference service. Some researchers visit facilities but many more write or telephone and ask assistance. Your institution should know what per cent of reference-staff time is devoted to written or telephonic service. If the same questions are raised — such as the hours and days open for business — a set of instructions or form letters should be printed for distribution. There should be no need to play twenty questions with researchers if the same questions and answers are involved time after time. Staff time is limited and valuable. Written procedures or guidelines for researchers are also valuable in providing guidance and on-the-job training for your staff. Managers and supervisors should be especially sensitive to the opportunities for printed information that can be sent by mail. A reference person would not force a researcher to wait two hours in order to search and answer a reference inquiry received the previous day.

It is essential that reference personnel understand the importance of the personal interview of the researcher. This step in the reference process is a crucial and demanding responsibility; however, an archivist or curator should have a positive attitude toward the person being interviewed. Care and attention should be given equally to both the well-known scholar and a person who wants information from the records of a local nineteenth-century business. Encourage the staff to view the personal interview of the researcher as an opportunity rather than an onerous task.

In the beginning of the interview the archivist should ask a series of questions which permits the researcher to define his or her subject. The archivist must be a good listener and ask questions which cause the visitor to define whether the topic is more extensive (scope) or more intensive (depth). If the researcher expects to do both, the interviewer must ask how much time the researcher expects to take using the records. The researcher may be unrealistic because of the volume of the records or manuscripts or the lack of finding aids. Share your view with the researcher, and tactfully suggest that it may not be possible to research everything he or she desires. In general, do not be afraid to make suggestions and offer advice. Final decisions, however, rest with the researcher. Because most searchers have limited research time at any one institution, it is wise, as a general rule, to provide him or her the series or records or manuscript collections which are most likely to yield pertinent information. If a researcher has almost unlimited time, direct him or her from the most probable to the least probable sources. An exceptional searcher may be willing to search your entire holdings. Remember that important historical documentation can be found in the most unlikely places. If the researcher insists on discounting reference-staff advice and desires to work in other collections, do not resist this. Few researchers will complain at the end if the reference person has outlined all the options during the interview.

The institution's reproduction procedures, fees and research rules should be explained at the outset. A sheet or brochure explaining these procedures is very useful and should include information pertaining to copyrighted material in the custody of the institution.

There are several functions comprising general reference service, but the two most important categories are information service and document service. Within information service, it is helpful to understand the difference between information from records or papers and information about records or papers.

If a staff person extracts the date of death of an individual from a personal-papers collection and supplies this information to the searcher, information from the record is furnished. It is simple to extract brief, factual data from documents. Names, dates, occupations or place names extracted from records can sometimes be placed within form letters especially designed to efficiently process high-volume, repetitive requests. A properly designed and correctly used form letter can save reference and clerical staff considerable amounts of time.

If, however, a historian asks an archivist to find what prompted a politician to make a particular speech or critical policy decision, the answer would be more difficult and the archivist would begin making judgments that only the researcher should make. Some reference persons forget that they are assisting the researcher and are not themselves acting as researcher. The public does not expect the reference librarian to know all the information contained in all the books in his library. Likewise, the researcher should not expect the archivist to know all the factual data in the records in his custody. The research public has a right to believe that the archivist knows as much about the records as possible. It is important to know about the finding aids to manuscript collections or archives. The most valuable finding aid, however, is the reference person—not a prepared guide, index or inventory. In many cases this most valuable finding aid evaluates and furnishes the prepared finding aids to the researcher. Knowing what major topics are included among records is very important because many researchers orient their research around major subjects, such as the American Revolution, Civil War, religion and transportation. A reference staff should constantly strive to gain additional knowledge about holdings. If donors impose restrictions on their personal papers, the reference person should be aware of this. Knowing how to obtain information about records or papers is very important.

The other major function involves making the records available. This includes bringing the records to the research room, making reproductions of records, and loaning of documents. It is wise not to make two series of records available to researchers at the same time. This will avoid the possibility of researchers mixing records from different agencies or offices. In addition, every request for records or papers should be indicated on a request form which best meets the institution's needs. The making of reproductions is a major responsibility of an institution's reference staff and cannot be taken lightly. Academic researchers are more likely to place large reproduction orders, and constant monitoring of such orders is needed to ensure accurate and prompt service.

Reference service is a dynamic, constantly changing relationship between researcher and archivist. There is one policy or principle, however, that should influence all reference activity. This has come to be called the policy of equal access. In 1973 the Society of American Archivists endorsed this policy. Briefly stated it proposes that all repositories of research materials make available their holdings on equal terms of access. This policy is well worth striving for in all repositories of historical documentation, but achieving it is quite difficult. The nature and mission of an institution will greatly affect the ability to attain this ideal. Private research institutions, financed by private funds, will more likely place priorities on certain types of requests. No institution — public or private — can avoid exceptions to the policy of equal access. Nevertheless, disregard of this practice will open your institution to charges of favoritism. The arbitrary or widespread disregard of equal access to documentation is also an intrusion on the tradition of scholarship.

The policy of equal access does not mean that any question asked should be answered. Most institutions must impose some limitations on what it considers legitimate reference service. These limitations must be applied consistently to all researchers. The first in importance is the ability of your archives to stop or limit reference services to someone who has violated user procedures made known when the person applied for research permission. The careless use of original materials or theft of documents are sufficient cause for withdrawal of the researcher-use privilege. Care should be used when this is done in order to avoid legal complications. Keep in mind, however, that the preservation of records must remain the first priority.

In the National Archives and Records Service, persons seeking general information relating to widely known events, persons or historical trends are referred to published works that are in a public or university library. The second limitation is that a reference staff should avoid doing substantive research for a requester. Admittedly, there is the question as to what constitutes substantive research, and every institution must define this area for its staff. In order to provide equal access it is sometimes necessary to limit the quantity of items per written or telephonic request. Obviously, a request that listed six hundred documents to be located and reproduced could be such a staff burden that other requests would be delayed or not answered. In order to process other requests and provide equal access, it might be necessary to inform the researcher that only thirty items were searched for and that subsequent requests be limited to thirty items. The standards set for quantity requests are arbitrary but they should apply equally.

Equal access must be set aside in special cases because of statutory requirements, court order, agency or corporate needs, overriding public interest, or the establishment of individual benefits. In this connection custodians of public records have special obligations. Both careful judgment and common sense must be considered if certain requests are moved ahead of requests received earlier.

In addition there are various restrictions of access, which can be placed into four general classes: statutory restrictions, governmental agency restrictions (federal, state, local), institutional restrictions, and donor-imposed restrictions. Any acquisition or accessioning program is predicated on the assumption that the documentation acquired will be used sooner or later. Archivists or manuscripts curators must honor such restrictions, but likewise they should work toward maximum release of materials as soon as possible.

The Freedom of Information Act of 1966 (amended in 1974) exempts from disclosure certain types of information found in records of the Executive Branch of the U.S. government. Other federal, state and local laws or regulations prohibit the release of other information or types of records.

Many private repositories have records or personal papers in their custody which document a private or confidential relationship. The personal papers of a lawyer might have information relating to the plea of a client in a felony case. Information given in confidence is a very sensitive issue and must be handled carefully. Any repository holding this type of documentation should have the capacity to develop and use restrictions. Few persons (corporations included) simply donate their materials to a repository without imposing some restrictions to access. These limitations should be a part of the deed of gift. Institutions acquiring personal-papers collections must weigh both the number and the time period of restrictions offered by donors. No hard-and-fast rule on how to make acquisitions can be designed.

It is important to know how to judge when reference service meets the high standards that it should. There are indicators that can be weighed. The protection and care an archives staff provides its holdings are very important. Careless and rough handling of records should not be permitted. Thoroughness in the reference service in your institution is another indicator which must be examined. If reproduction orders are carelessly processed, and follow-up letters are never written, reference supervisors must take action. Courtesy to the researcher is a consistent hallmark of high-quality reference service. Archivists and manuscript curators make documentation available in a prompt and professional manner. This does not mean, however, that the reference person is a servant of the researcher and that he or she must do what the researcher desires. Firmness is sometimes a very important quality in relating to difficult researchers.

Another indicator of professional-quality reference service is the cooperation that takes place among the institution's reference staff. Staff members should help each other voluntarily and share their particular strengths when performing reference service. Widespread rivalry or professional jealousy does little to build staff *esprit* and usually breaks down communication among the staff. Usually the research clientele suffers.

The last indicator is the recognition by researchers of reference services performed. This may take many forms—a sincere but short statement of appreciation when a researcher finishes, or a thank-you note or letter to

the archivist or to the director of your institution. By word of mouth, researchers will urge others to visit your facility or warn them to stay away if
their experiences were unpleasant. In some cases researchers will acknowl-
edge their debt to archivists in their publications. Some authors will send a
complimentary copy of their book or article to the reference person along
with a personalized inscription: The composite recognition of an institution's reference services is very important and must be evaluated constantly.

In conclusion an institution must be committed to the goal of making its
documentary resources available to its clientele in a professional and ex-
peditious manner. This committment to research and a better grasp of the
human past must motivate those who make our documentary heritage
available. Striving toward this goal is a constant duty.

Security

By Edmund Berkeley, Jr.

SECURITY is a primary concern of archivists because they are charged with the preservation of those manuscript collections or institutional records that are of enduring value to their employers, whether those employers are large state archives, small private historical societies, business archives, or any of the many other types of modern archival institutions. Allowing valuable holdings to deteriorate — or to be stolen — violates the canon of preservation with which archivists are charged. In recent years, theft has become a major problem for archivists; many institutions, large and small, have suffered thefts, and it seems likely that this trend will continue unless archivists take appropriate steps to reduce the possibilities.

Archival theft has existed as long as man has kept records; in ancient times, one of the spoils of war was frequently the records of the defeated. Dr. Joseph Fields has written:

> Ptolemy Philadelphus is supposed to have refused to supply wheat to the starving Athenians, caught in the ravages of a famine, unless he was permitted to borrow the manuscripts of the Greek literary and philosophical giants so that he might have copies made. He is said to have retained the originals and sent the copies back to Athens.

The great library of Alexandria, one of the wonders of the ancient world, was the private library of the ptolemies, and most of its contents had been captured from defeated enemies. Nineteenth-century manuscripts collectors apparently learned from Ptolemy Philadelphus. Many of the great manuscripts collectors of that period simply "borrowed" manuscripts and "forgot" to return them. A number of famous collections now in well-known institutions have very questionable provenances for this reason.

During the past four decades theft from archival institutions has accelerated. Clippings in the files of the Manuscripts Department of the University of Virginia Library tell of many incidents. Philip P. Mason, the archivist most knowledgeable about archival theft, summarized the statistics in an article entitled, "Archival Security: New Solutions to an Old Problem," published in the October, 1975, *American Archivist*:

---

* Joseph E. Fields, "The History of Autograph Collecting," in Edmund Berkeley, Jr., *ed. Autographs and Manuscripts: A Collector's Manual* (New York: Charles Scribner's Sons, 1978), p. 42.

During the past decade several hundred archives and libraries have been victimized and many others have been and did not report it. The recent loss of the Felix Frankfurter diaries and papers from the Manuscript Division of the Library of Congress capped a series of thefts from that institution and led to a complete revamping of its security regulations. The thefts of valuable archival materials from the University of Virginia, the Detroit Public Library, North Carolina State Archives, Texas State Archives, Wayne State University, Yale University, Franklin D. Roosevelt Library, Indiana State Library, Ohio Historical Society, Virginia State Archives, State Historical Society of Wisconsin, and the National Archives demonstrate the dimensions of the problem.

Mason also summarizes the reasons for archival theft. He notes that some persons have a strong desire to gain possession of certain manuscripts because they feel that the institution and its employees cannot appreciate the manuscripts as much as they do. Kleptomania and the challenge of beating the security systems figure in other cases. Some thieves want to "borrow" records "temporarily" because having them in their possession will "facilitate" their research. Other thieves desire to purge records by removing them because they contain something damaging to them or their families. And still others remove records because they have some connection with an ancestor.

There are other reasons for archival theft. There is today a large number of highly educated persons who have little or no respect for personal or public property, and who have or know how to acquire the specialized knowledge necessary to steal from archives. Certain thefts are committed by persons who have grievances against the institution or against its employees. And there are a certain number of thefts for which there is no obvious reason, since the material does not appear on the market and is not recovered.

Perhaps the most important reason for archival theft is profit. Philip P. Mason firmly believes that profit is the basic reason for most archival theft, and he has assembled much evidence to support his contention. The thefts in recent years from the North Carolina, Georgia, Texas and California archives were all committed in order to market the stolen documents. Dealer-auctioneer Charles Hamilton has written most engagingly of his own experiences with forgers and thieves in *Scribblers and Scoundrels*; he has been instrumental in apprehending a number of each.

All collectible items — stamps, silver, gold, art, rare books, manuscripts, and so on — enjoy rising prices in times of prosperity, such as the 1970s. When materials in a field of collecting, such as manuscripts, begin to show a spectacular rate of appreciation, many persons with excess cash enter the collecting field, and some are not ethical. If such speculators learn of items that they want to acquire for their collections and find that they cannot acquire these items legally, they will take other steps to acquire them. The thieves convicted of the theft from the North Carolina archives told state bureau of investigation personnel that manuscripts could be stolen to order.

Prominent manuscripts dealer Kenneth W. Rendell believes that profit is not a major reason for archival theft. He has stated publicly that "only a very small percentage of the stolen material eventually comes onto the market." He is referring to the major market for manuscripts in which he and perhaps five other firms handle about ninety per cent of the business. Stolen manuscripts move in small local markets; the material stolen from the Georgia archives was recovered from an Atlanta flea market. Rendell is critical of archivists for failing to take sufficient steps to protect their holdings from theft, particularly by marking holdings to show ownership. He also faults those archivists and others who will not admit and publicize a theft, for he believes that publicity makes it more difficult for a thief to sell stolen property. Publicity also alerts dealers who might otherwise quite innocently purchase stolen property.

Whatever the reasons, archival theft is flourishing. Every archivist must take steps to protect the holdings of his or her institution and must plan what must be done if a theft is suspected or discovered.

Appended to this article is a lengthy security checklist (Appendix IV). Using such a list is a good way to assess the security of an institution and its archivists' awareness of security problems that it may have. Not all of the questions on the checklist will apply to every institution, but many of them are basic to any archives or manuscripts repository and its operation.

In thinking about the security of an institution, the archivist should remember that its staff is the institution's best security system. Convincing the staff of the necessity for constant awareness of security will do more to improve the level of security provided its records or collections than any amount of money spent on electronic security systems. A good level of security has been achieved when the staff questions everything out of the ordinary, from the furtive patron to the mysterious "buzzing" of a light switch that may mean a loose electrical connection — a potential fire hazard. The staff member who notices a peculiar smell in a stack area, investigates, and finds that the janitor has left a pile of oily rags that are beginning to smoulder will have more than repaid the archivist for the time and effort spent on a security program.

Unfortunately, staff members also pose a considerable security risk to the institution. The staff has access to most security areas in the institution and it is usually easy for its members to remove materials from the building or archives area of the building. Ultimately, considerable faith must be placed in the staff; however, make as many basic checks on new staff members as possible, and establish certain rules that will give a minimum level of security against theft by staff members. Credentials of all new staff members should be checked carefully. Do not permit staff members to collect materials in the same areas in which the institution specializes, as collecting is a mysterious disease that can cause a person to lose normal restraints and can, through conflicts of interest, cause problems for a staff member involved in collecting work for the institution. If possible and affordable, it is a good idea to bond staff members both for performance and surety. A surety bond requires a thorough background check by the bonding agency, and the mere mention in interviews of such a background check has brought forth useful information to interviewers. If possible, archives staff members should be paid adequately and all staff grievances handled promptly and thoroughly. Avoid student and volunteer help unless these persons are closely supervised and are forbidden access to the high-security areas of the institution.

The patrons of an archives probably pose the greatest threat. There have been after-hours burglaries in archives, but the number is much smaller than the number of thefts committed by patrons in archives reading rooms. The North Carolina, Georgia and Texas state archives all suffered thefts from well-staffed reading rooms. The reality of the situation is that any institution is running a considerable risk when a non-staff member uses its holdings. Because archivists want the holdings in their institutions to be used by the public — or whatever their constituency is — they must compromise security to a degree when holdings are used. Perhaps if archivists required patrons to strip and wear pocketless coveralls into the reading room and subjected them to a complete body search before returning their clothes, the risk of theft from reading rooms might be reduced considerably. Given the conventions of today's society, archivists must meet the threat without such Draconian measures.

The archivist must obtain basic information about the patrons who use his holdings by requiring each one to complete a comprehensive registration form. A staff member should interview each new patron to serve the dual purposes of security and good reference service.

Basic reading-room security demands that the room never be left unattended while patrons are using holdings. Limit the amount of material each patron may have at any one time. Do not allow patrons to take brief cases, handbags or similar containers to research tables, and search all note paper used by patrons before they leave the reading room. Use a collection request form that has at least two parts: file one by the date the collection was used, and the second by the name or accession number of the collection. These two files will enable you to determine quickly who used a specific collection on a given date, or who last used the collection. Both pieces of information may be vital should you discover something missing. Train staff members assigned to the reading room to provide both good service and good security. Do not require so much regular work of reading-room staff that they must neglect these vital functions. Establish a definite procedure to be followed by a staff member who observes a patron concealing a document under clothing.

To prepare a procedure for the staff to follow in the case of suspected or observed theft, it is best to have the advice of an attorney. If legal services are not available, the local law enforcement agency may be helpful as many police departments have outreach programs, and it may also be able to consult the local district attorney for advice about recommended procedures. If the law enforcement agency sends an officer or team to inspect the archives to make recommendations about security, it will prove mutually beneficial as few police officers have any knowledge of archives and their special security problems.

Increasing security in a reading room usually requires no outlay of funds. Researchers who object to new and tighter security regulations should be informed of the rash of archival thefts and that the duty of the archives staff is to safeguard the archives' holdings. Usually, patrons are quite interested in the steps taken to ensure that the holdings will be there for future consultation. Improvements in perimeter security for after-hours protection should certainly be made if possible. Some perimeter electronic security systems are inexpensive if the archives has staff members with the technical knowledge and skills necessary to install them, for the major cost of such systems is in the labor.

Because of the threat to archives posed by the large number of thefts in recent years, the Society of American Archivists (SAA) applied for and was awarded a grant from the National Endowment for the Humanities (NEH) to fund a four-phase program on archival theft. First, SAA established a register of stolen and missing archival materials; it is updated several times a year and mailed to over twelve hundred manuscripts dealers and to many archivists in the United States and abroad. This register makes it much more difficult to market stolen archival materials because most dealers will check it before purchasing materials from persons unknown to them. The register has also been useful in the recovery of some stolen manuscripts. Registration forms may be obtained from the SAA Archival Security Program, 330 South Wells Street, Suite 810, Chicago, Illinois 60606.

The second phase of the NEH grant program finances an archival security newsletter, published bi-monthly as part of the SAA *Newsletter*. It carries timely notices of interest to persons concerned with archival security. A third phase of the grant program was the preparation of an archival-security manual as one in the SAA basic archival manuals series. This manual should be acquired from SAA by any security-conscious archives or archivist. A consultants' program was established by the grant that allows an institution desiring the services of an archival-security expert to obtain one through SAA. Normally, the institution pays the consultant's travel and other expenses while the SAA program pays the honorarium. Archivists interested in a visit by a consultant should also consult the archival-security program director at the address above. Consultants from all types of archival agencies, from the large public to the smallest private, are available. The results of this phase of the program have been quite satisfactory.

A fifth area of interest for the SAA archival-security program evolved from the program itself. This is a model-laws program. One of the most difficult situations faced by an archivist in protecting holdings is that created when a patron is observed or suspected of having concealed a document that he or she has been using. A confrontation over this concealment involves several controversial areas of modern law, such as search and seizure and privacy. The SAA model law, if adapted to fit a state's legal code, and passed by its legislature, provides the archivist—and the librarian—the protection offered in a number of states to a merchant who confronts a shopper suspected of shoplifting; that is, if the archivist or librarian acts on the best information available and proceeds in a proper and prescribed fashion so as not to violate any of the rights of the suspect, he or she cannot be the subject of a civil suit arising from a false accusation. This law, first passed in Virginia through the efforts of the University of Virginia Library, has been adopted by six other states, and is before legislative committees in several others. As Pennsylvania law does not presently provide such protection for its archivists, it would certainly be a good idea for Pennsylvania archivists to consider working for passage of this law in their state.* A copy of the model law may be obtained from the SAA archival-security office, that also can advise anyone about the best procedure to follow in dealing with a legislature.

Security for the holdings of any archives is an important responsibility of the archivists of its staff. No institution may consider itself immune to the threat of theft. Every archivist must familiarize himself or herself with the security procedures of the institution for which he or she works, and must improve them if necessary and if possible. Archivists must be ever-vigilant to preserve the records and collections of their institutions for future generations.

---

* The Pennsylvania Historical and Museum Commission and the Pennsylvania State Library are working for the adoption of such legislation (1979).

Storage, Space and Equipment

By Samuel Mauray

T HE necessary ingredient for effective utilization of your space and equipment is planning. And because the circumstances and needs of each location are different, one must consider a general approach to reviewing these important but often overlooked aspects of archival and historical administration.

Step 1. It is vital that professionals determine what their needs are. One cannot afford to be sidetracked by wishful thinking, and, therefore, must be practical in determining what are essential needs in the short run and what can realistically be expected in the future. Normally, a five-year projection will be satisfactory for this purpose, but there may be factors which could make it desirable to plan for a longer period of time. Your space and equipment forecasts should furthermore be flexible to allow for interim changes in your operation.

In assessing space needs one must be able to provide some answers to six essential questions. These are:

What kinds of materials are involved (i.e., bound volumes, diaries, manuscripts, maps, microfilm, negatives, newspapers, photographs, prints, recordings)?

What are the sizes of the various materials?

What are the current volumes of each of the materials and what is the future increase or decrease likely to be?

How are the materials arranged or sequenced?

Do the materials require special handling or environmental control? How much and what kinds of equipment and supplies do you need for the respective materials?

Step 2. Once you have determined your needs, you should inventory your equipment. List each piece of equipment, its size and any other pertinent data, such as capacity, electrical requirements, or condition, if appropriate. Use this information and the date compiled on equipment in step one to determine your equipment needs. Some areas also worth reviewing are:

How much of your short and long term needs can be met with your present equipment?

If you must obtain additional equipment what will you need and when?

Can any additional equipment be obtained from some surplus source or must it be purchased?

Will you have the money to buy equipment when you need it?

Some equipment considerations are (i.e., library shelving, storage shelving, vaults/safes, storage cabinets, bookcases, microfilm readers or reader-printers, file cabinets, map cabinets or racks, electro-mechanical equipment such as Kardveyers or Elektrievers, work and reference tables, office equipment, supplies — storage boxes, file folders.

Once compiled this inventory should be kept and updated as you add or delete equipment.

Step 3. This step has two phases. First, prepare a layout of your space (see Exhibit 1). Use graph paper, preferably one-fourth inch, to draw a floor plan of your facility. Pay special attention to:

natural light — show window locations and sizes
artificial light — indicate location and kind of light fixtures
electrical outlets — indicate 2 or 3 prong
telephone outlets
door locations and sizes
built-in furniture — bookcases, counters, etc.

Secondly, prepare templates of all your present and proposed equipment (see Exhibit 2). These should be to the same scale as your floor plan. Write the name of the equipment type on each template. You may want to use different-colored paper to distinguish between the equipment that you now have and that which you expect to acquire in the future.

Step 4. After you have done the above, the time is right to fit all the pieces together! Take your layout and equipment templates and begin to develop alternate layouts. (See Exhibits 3, 4 and 5.) It is usually best to work with the larger or heavier pieces of equipment first as well as those requiring special considerations such as electrical or telephone connections. Some special considerations are:

Security. Early in the process decide which areas are going to be used by the public and then arrange the furniture and equipment to allow for visual and physical control of the visitors.

Sound. Place any equipment such as typewriters, microfilm readers or reader-printers in a location that will cause the least disturbance to your visitors.

Eye appeal. A cluttered area indicates a lack of organization. Attempt to maintain a feeling of openness and efficiency. Place the taller pieces of equipment against a wall or out of the general work or reference area.

Aisles. Provide sufficient aisle width to provide for the easy movement of materials and people.

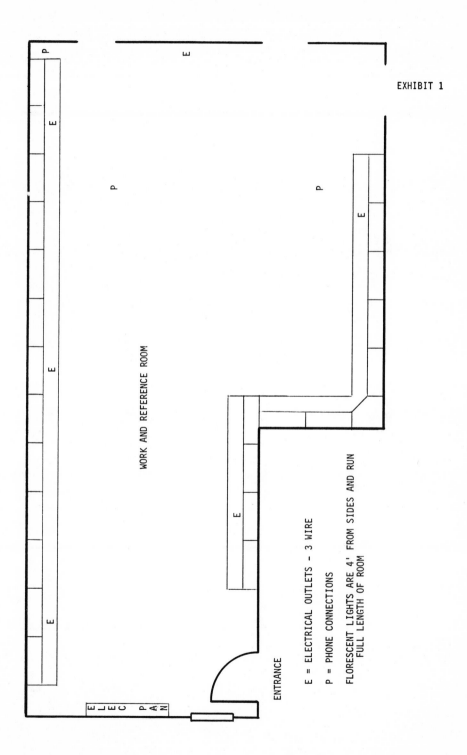

EXHIBIT 1

WORK AND REFERENCE ROOM

ENTRANCE

E = ELECTRICAL OUTLETS - 3 WIRE

P = PHONE CONNECTIONS

FLORESCENT LIGHTS ARE 4' FROM SIDES AND RUN
FULL LENGTH OF ROOM

EXHIBIT 2

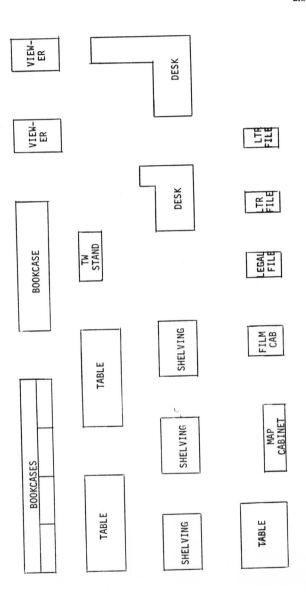

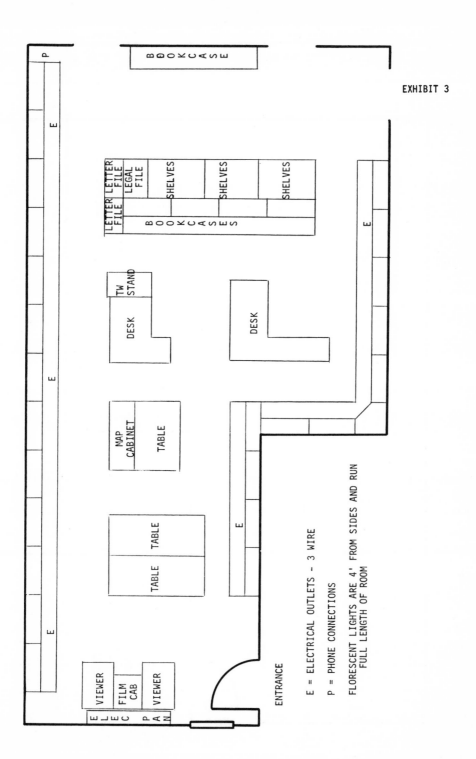

EXHIBIT 3

BOOKCASE

LETTER FILE | LETTER FILE | LEGAL FILE | SHELVES | SHELVES | SHELVES

BOOKCASES

TW STAND

DESK

DESK

MAP CABINET

TABLE

TABLE | TABLE

TABLE

VIEWER

FILM CAB

VIEWER

E L E C | P A N

ENTRANCE

E = ELECTRICAL OUTLETS - 3 WIRE

P = PHONE CONNECTIONS

FLORESCENT LIGHTS ARE 4' FROM SIDES AND RUN
FULL LENGTH OF ROOM

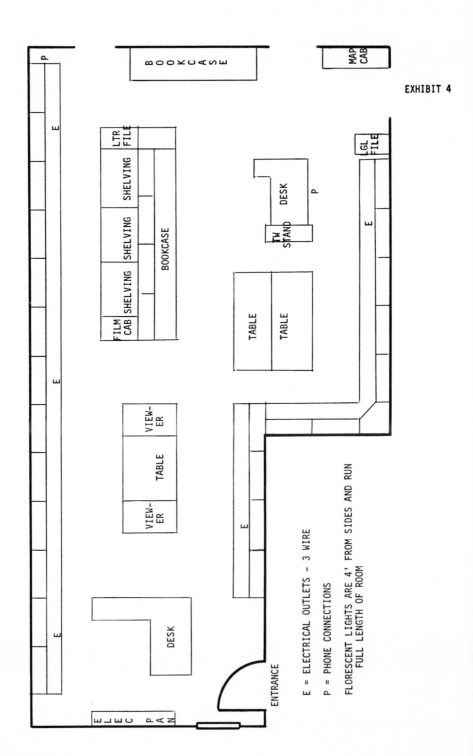

EXHIBIT 4

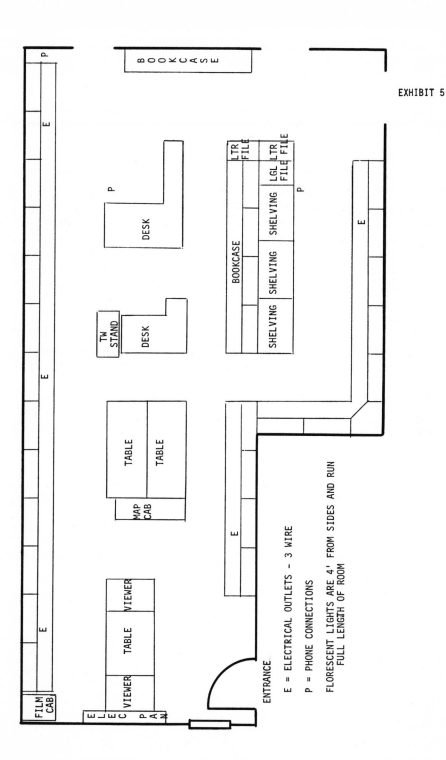

EXHIBIT 5

ENTRANCE

E = ELECTRICAL OUTLETS - 3 WIRE

P = PHONE CONNECTIONS

FLORESCENT LIGHTS ARE 4' FROM SIDES AND RUN
FULL LENGTH OF ROOM

Equipment size. Be certain to check door or window sizes so that you can get any additional equipment into your facility.

The objective of this phase is to select the best possible configuration of furniture and equipment taking into consideration the normal constraints of manpower, money, space and time. There are two points to keep in mind: First, your final decision should not be based solely on minimum cost. Secondly, your final choice will quite likely be a compromise, usually caused by one or more of the above constraints.

Step 5. Once you have determined your course of action in step 4, it is time to start planning your implementation. Prepare a list of what must be done and when it is to be done, to arrive at the necessary steps to be taken. These lists should also be used to monitor the implementation.

If your operation will be going through some major changes during the planning period, you may want to divide the implementation into several sub-phases, based on equipment additions or deletions, space availability or accessions.

It seems unnecessary to say that your layout and equipment have a great deal to do with the level of service that you provide. However, day-to-day pressures are too often permitted to crowd out the planning which is an absolute necessity if you are to make use of your facility and equipment.

To maintain an effective and efficient operation you must periodically review your needs and services. The results will be in direct proportion to the effort you expend.

Part 4

THE CONSERVATION
AND PRESERVATION
OF HISTORICAL MATERIALS

Prevention and Preservation Techniques

Disasters: Can We Plan
For Them?
If Not, How Can We Proceed?

By Willman Spawn

Between 1955 and 1965, approximately 340 accidents to libraries involving damage by fire, water, hurricanes and internal plumbing have been recorded in the United States alone." This startling figure comes from an unpublished report by Peter Waters of the Library of Congress Preservation Office. In 1966 this figure was eclipsed by a single event, the floods of Florence, when a million and a half books and newspapers in the National Library of Italy were damaged by water, mud and oil, and eight hundred thousand vellum and paper manuscripts were damaged in the National Archives. The financial loss was staggering, the intellectual loss no less so; however, the floods provided an unexpected opportunity when conservators convened from around the world to work, to exchange information and ideas, and ultimately to improve the methods of handling water-damaged materials.

The knowledge thus gained has been put to good use since 1966. In Pennsylvania alone, during the past dozen years there have been many cases of water damage, some involving whole libraries. It is obvious that water damage is not an isolated or unusual phenomenon, and that preventive measures are well worth the cost, which in the long run is less than the cost of the cure.

Two printed manuals mark the progress made in the last few years in dealing with disasters. The first, a pamphlet which appeared in 1972, is entitled *Procedures for Salvage of Water-damaged Library Materials*, by Peter Waters. The second, published in April, 1978, is *Disaster Prevention and Disaster Preparedness*, by Hilda Bohem, associate librarian of the University of California, Los Angeles, and a member of the University of California Task Group on the Preservation of Library Materials. These two manuals should be read and heeded by anyone with even a passing interest in their subjects, for each packs a great deal of essential advice into a clear, concise format. Mrs. Bohem's manual, in particular, is a pioneering effort in an untravelled field. If every librarian made a serious effort to follow her recommendations, the "disaster business" would diminish considerably.

In order to keep the subject of disaster prevention to a manageable size, I will ask you to assume that the disaster could or did occur to a single library building and not to an entire system or locality. We are speculating about a fire, a leaky roof, a clogged drain, and not about an earthquake or a tidal wave. After all, the difference between a localized and a general disaster is only one of complexity; the basic rules remain the same.

RULE NUMBER ONE in disaster prevention is "know your building"— know its history, its flaws, its potential problems. The following checklist is divided into subject areas; while it may be incomplete, it provides a good start in getting to know your physical plant.

History How old is your building? Has it ever had a fire or a case of water damage? If so, were the causes of the disaster removed or only patched over? Could it happen again in the same place, in the same way?

Layout Do you have a set of plans for the building, showing not only its design but the placement of plumbing and mechanical and electrical systems? Is it up to date?

Water How old is the roof? Are there any signs of leaks, new or old? Are the drains and the downspouts regularly checked for clogging or breaks? Is there a skylight that might leak?

Are the windows tight? Are windows ever left open for ventilation, so that a hard rain could come in and damage nearby material?

Are you vulnerable to rising water at ground level? Could a flash flood or flooding river water enter the building? Are there ever signs of seepage in the basement after a heavy or prolonged rain? Have you ever needed to use a pump to remove moisture from the basement? Is there a smell of mildew anywhere in the building in humid weather?

Do you have steam heat or an old hot-water system? If the answer is yes, do the pipes pass above the book stacks? Do your plumbing lines run near the book stacks? If a pipe breaks or a toilet overflows, do you know where to cut off the water supply?

Power Where is your fuse box or master panel? Is it locked, and if so where is the key kept? Does more than one person know the key's location? Are there electrical outlets in the stacks? Are the power lines heavy duty where needed, or is the system possibly over-loaded by today's demands?

If the power fails due to a disaster, even a minor one, do you have an alternate power source? Where would you get one if needed? How much power (i.e., how many amps) would you need from a portable generator? Remember, wet books and papers need to be kept cold to inhibit mold growth; how much power would you need for this?

Fire   Do you have the appropriate fire extinguishers located conveniently throughout the library? Have staff members ever actually used an extinguisher, or have they only read the directions? Have you ever had a fire drill with emphasis on saving books as well as people? Does the Fire Marshal inspect the building regularly, and if he finds violations, are they corrected or only white-washed?

RULE NUMBER TWO in disaster prevention relates to your storage arrangements. Do you have an up-to-date diagram of each stack level, showing the location of major subject areas and indicating the inclusive call numbers? Where is your most valuable material stored? Do you have your art books, your films, photographs, microfilms and microfiches stored in the basement or up under the roof? Both these locations are especially vulnerable to water damage. If you have a locked storage area, are the keys readily available and their location known to all the staff? If this storage area is seldom entered and contains its own air conditioning unit, is the area checked daily to make sure the unit is operating correctly?

Finally, RULE NUMBER THREE deals with staff participation in disaster prevention. Can all off-duty staff members be alerted quickly in case of an emergency? Has one person been designated as an emergency coordinator? (This person need not be the library director, but it should be someone known for common sense, a calm manner and a flexible mind.) Is the coordinator prepared to deal with a disaster, and does he or she have a group of staff members prepared to assist? In Bohem's terminology, this group would be called the disaster action team, or DAT, with responsibility for preparedness, salvage and post-mortem operations.

Before the discussion turns from prevention to preparedness, I would like to stress that "an ounce of prevention is [still] worth a pound of cure." In only twenty years, Pennsylvania libraries have sustained water damage fromvkeat variety of causes—a clogged roof drain, a broken steam pipe, overflow from a washroom sink, condensation inside a building from excessive humidity, flooding after a hurricane, the extinguishing of a fire. One or two of these causes, the hurricane for example, could be considered as "acts of God" and not preventable, but there is no doubt that adequate prevention could have reduced their impact and saved hundreds of hours of staff time and thousands of dollars spent on salvage.

Yet, one must be realistic, especially in this world of shrinking budgets and galloping inflation. There are only a few libraries that will be able to set up a prevention and preparedness program of any size. Consequently, certain simple and inexpensive procedures that can ease the impact of a disaster should be examined and recommended as a start.

First of all, obtain a number of copies of the Bohem and Waters manuals, and make sure that the entire staff reads and digests them. Then discuss the Bohem recommendations for prevention and preparedness at one or more staff meetings, inviting criticisms and suggestions. The Bohem recommendations may seem over-elaborate for a small library, but personal experience suggests that they can be adapted to a library of almost any size.

Second, set up a disaster action team, which should include staff members with knowledge of the building, the collections and outside resources. It may well be that the staff people who demonstrated the quickest comprehension of the Bohem recommendations and the need for them will be the initial members of your disaster action team.

Third, select one staff member as recovery director or emergency coordinator, whichever title suits your circumstances better. In the past, this person usually has been the outside expert brought in to supervise the salvage operation. As the expert in the field, the outsider has a distinct advantage: his decisions are treated as gospel—at least as long as he is on the spot! However, such an expert is not always available, and his services usually require a fee. Therefore, it seems advantageous to train a staff member as a resident specialist, or at least as a person capable of recognizing the problems and arranging for the appropriate solutions.

This selection will put a great deal of responsibility on the shoulders of an already overburdened staff member. But the resident specialist starts with some advantages of his or her own: knowledge of the building and its history, awareness of the strengths and weaknesses of the staff, contacts with possible resources in the surrounding area. The specialist can expand these advantages by reading the literature, attending workshops and conferences on prevention and salvage, and adapting the knowledge gained to his or her specific situation. In the words of Bohem,

> If the Recovery Director is a staff member, it shall be his responsibility to keep thoroughly informed and up to date on disaster recovery techniques and to make an annual report to the DAT so that they will have a general familiarity with the latest procedures. It shall also be the Director's responsibility to assemble a reference library of disaster literature to be available to the DAT for their further education and as reference during a crisis. An

updated list of persons who may be contacted for expert advice in
an emergency. . .should be part of this reference material.

The following items are essential in preparing to deal with the results of
a disaster:

1) up-to-date copies of a telephone list of the disaster action team, desig-
   nating their functions (i.e., director, cataloguer, cleaner);
2) a "telephone tree" of library staff members so that the entire staff can
   be alerted quickly to a crisis;
3) **a list of resources, including the police and fire officials, who could
   authorize emergency parking, pumping, etc.; suppliers of such items
   as plastic crates, deep-freeze facilities, portable pumps, generators
   and fans;**
4) a list of possible volunteer helpers from other libraries, community
   groups, library organizations, past staff members and others;
5) an arrangement for paying the bills for emergency needs which by-
   passes the usual library routine; this arrangement can be vital when
   quick decisions and instant availability can determine the success or
   failure of a salvage operation.

The salvage operation will gain nothing by hasty action or by riding
roughshod over staff members who may be in a state of shock. For a dedi-
cated librarian there can be no shock comparable to finding two feet of
water in the basement on Monday morning, or watching water drip from
the ceiling onto the rare-book collection below. Planning will help you and
your staff regain the confidence to cope with the unexpected crisis. People
suddenly faced with an overwhelming burden can find unsuspected
strength when given time to pull themselves together. This will be
especially true if they can rely on knowledge previously gained.

A nucleus of reference books on disaster management already exists.
These include the pamphlets cited above by Waters and Bohem, and the
author's "After the Water Comes," which appeared in the 1973 issue of the
Pennsylvania Library Association Bulletin, devoted to preservation of
library materials. (Other items are listed in the appended bibliography.)
The specific procedures, cautions and recommendations included in these
printed statements are easily read and comprehended, and need not be re-
stated here. However, there are some general rules that are always worth
repetition.

When disaster strikes, most individuals feel a tremendous urge to "do
something." By the law of averages, the right thing is often done—but not
always. In fact, hasty or uninformed action may complicate the very situation it sets out to save. There is little to be gained by haste and everything
to be gained by establishing the dimensions of the problem. Has the cause
of the disaster been determined and has it been dealt with adequately?

What types of materials are involved? How many books will need to be handled? Who will coordinate the arrival of the packing crates, the volunteers, the refrigerated van? If it is a holiday, a weekend, or a summer vacation time, can the expected resources be relied upon?

An aspect of salvage that is often overlooked is the need to record the operation from the very beginning: the circumstances, the decisions, the staff involved and so on. It is unwise to rely on memory for these factors during a crisis, especially if insurance claims are to be made. Most salvage operations stretch over many months, and careful records will prove their worth many times over. Meticulous records *must* be kept of the handling of the books; therefore, a cataloguer is included on the disaster action team from its inception. A diary will help to avoid duplication of effort; it will provide the basis for judging what parts of the operation were well handled, and which need improvement for the future; it can serve as the foundation for reports to be made to trustees, library groups and other agencies. In Bohem's words,

> Publication should be considered because the more we learn about other people's methods of coping with disaster, the better prepared we can be for our own. It behooves us to share our experience.

If you need to call in an outside consultant to act as the recovery director or to advise your staff specialist, he or she will need plenty of hard facts in order to make the right decisions. (Here the diary will be invaluable.) The consultant cannot begin to know your collection as well as you do, viz., which items can be replaced and which are irreplaceable; which items get limited use and can wait for care while others must receive priority attention; which items can be discarded immediately. Teamwork, combining your local knowledge with his technical knowledge, usually produces a successful result at the lowest possible cost.

A final word. The recovery director must be the authority whether he is an outside consultant or a resident specialist. As Bohem writes, "It is essential. . .that final decision making be centered in one authoritative person." An extraordinary situation calls for an extraordinary solution: individual rights and conflicts may have to be submerged for a time in order for the director and his team to function for the common good. The ultimate success of the salvage operation will depend on the cooperation they receive.

First Steps in Preservation
For Small Archives
And Historical Societies

By Norvell Jones

CONSERVATION and preservation of collection material is a major concern for small archives and historical societies. The custodians charged with the care of these collections usually are faced with administering a large quantity of historical material and hopelessly inadequate budgets. Furthermore, trained conservators are hard to find and professional treatment is often expensive. In spite of this rather grim outlook, there is much that can and must be done to insure the preservation of a collection on a daily basis. An enlightened, common-sense approach to the handling and storage of collections is a prerequisite to preservation, and without this foundation no amount of deacidification or restoration treatment can insure survival.

Listed below are seven points that will be helpful to custodians in preserving their collections on a day-to-day basis and establishing long-range preservation priorities. While these guidelines do not cover all the specific problems faced by institutions, it is hoped that they will stimulate thought and suggest possible solutions.

1. *Provide the Best Environment You Can Afford*

Archival material is damaged by exposure to light, heat, fluctuations in relative humidity, and atmospheric pollution. The amount of control possible in a small institution will depend on geography, type of building, and budget. Even the smaller institution can do something in this area.

The damaging properties of light can be controlled most easily. Since any visible light may be damaging, where light is not needed it can simply be eliminated. Storage areas can be darkened when not in use by blocking windows and keeping electric lights turned off. The ultraviolet portion, which is greatest in direct sunlight and fluorescent light, is the most damaging portion of visible light. When fluorescent lights are being used, the tubes should be fully covered with ultraviolet filtering sleeves. Work areas and search rooms which are lit most of the time should have window blinds or curtains that can be closed to reduce direct sunlight. Incandescent lights present more danger from the heat they generate than from

77

ultraviolet radiation. When they are used they should be positioned far enough from collection-material work surfaces so that they do not heat the items.

Heat damages archival material by speeding degradation reactions. Generally, the lowest temperatures possible in small institutions with working collections are almost always 70 ± 5 °F, the temperatures at which people are most comfortable. Naturally, lower temperatures will help material last longer. When summer temperatures are higher than 70 to 75 °F, air conditioning should be given a high budget priority in order to extend the life of the collections.

Fluctuations in relative humidity are also damaging to archival material, but are extremely difficult and expensive to control. A relative humidity close to fifty per cent is good for most items housed in small repositories. A humidifier connected to the heating system in winter and a dehumidifier for high humidity areas in the summer will help, but they cannot provide the critical control to 50 ± 5 per cent achieved by some sophisticated air conditioning systems.

Airborne pollution is difficult to eliminate without air scrubbers in a total air conditioning system. Small institutions should be sure that filters in the heating and cooling systems are cleaned and checked periodically. To protect collection material from pollution, use storage folders and boxes which incorporate alkaline-buffered paper. Such containers will be beneficial even in areas where chemical pollution is not a major problem by protecting from dust and physical damage. These commercially available folders and boxes will also cut down on acid migration from inherently bad paper within the collections.

Careful planning of storage and work areas can reduce damage to material in a working collection. Provide adequate shelving, preferably metal with no sharp edges, to accommodate the usual-size boxes and bound volumes in your collection. Oversize material requires special thought. Because of size it is awkward to handle and especially vulnerable to damage. In addition to special deep shelving and oversize drawers, allow for aisles wide enough for your largest items, and, if at all possible, provide empty shelves at regular intervals and flat surfaces to make moving large items as painless as possible. Work surfaces should be as large as is practical and should be kept clear of everything except work in progress. Crowding is the source of much accidental damage. When work areas are separated from storage areas by more than a few feet, some sort of truck is essential. The design and type will depend on your collection.

2. *Always Handle Collection Material As Though It Were Vulnerable*

Everything in your collection is handled, first when it is processed and later when it is stored or used. At each step there are dangers which must be avoided.

When you are dealing with historical materials do not overestimate your strength or ability. Strong material, in good condition, is not especially vulnerable when handled with care; however, heavy items and large stacks of books or folders will be damaged if they are dropped. Request help with heavy awkward items; if help is not available wait until it is. Make extra trips or use a truck when there is more than you should carry. The time it takes for a second trip is less than that required to repair even one item.

Material which is damaged, brittle or already fractured is often identified for the first time during processing, the ideal time to prevent further damage. But no matter when such material is discovered, you should take steps immediately to minimize future damage and provide safer handling.

The first concern is to support and protect the item. For thin, unbound items which are brittle or badly torn, transparent polyester film is ideal. Two pieces of film cut to a standard size are joined on one edge with a piece of double-coated tape. (See photograph.) This protective "processing folder" allows a very vulnerable item to be handled without further damage. A supply of these folders should be available in processing areas. In many instances the item can be stored permanently in the folder. For large, heavy or inflexible items which may be cracked or are likely to break from their own weight, a rigid support is essential. A corrugated-cardboard sandwich can be used temporarily to immobilize and transport such material, but corrugated board is acid and should not be in direct contact with the item. For long-term storage, alkaline conservation board should

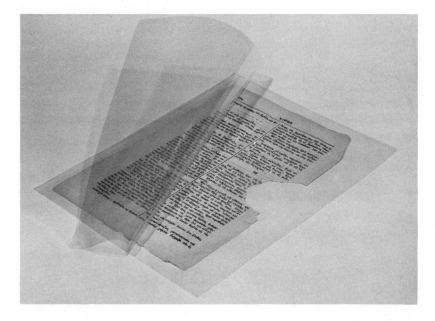

be used either as a mat or folder to provide proper support and protect the item.

For bound volumes or pamphlets which are damaged, vulnerable or have loose parts, use some sort of folded wrapper which you can make yourself. The Library of Congress phase box made from alkaline-lined board is a very sturdy possibility. Instructions for making this box are available on request. The American Philosophical Society folder, which was developed by Willman Spawn, is also an excellent choice and somewhat easier to make. Instructions are given with the diagram on page 81. These folders protect the items from dust and light as well as physical damage.

Some materials are inherently unstable. Newsprint and other acidic paper containing lignin, some Thermofax copies, concentrated iron-gall ink, and cellulose nitrate film are a few examples. Efforts to stabilize them seldom are completely successful. Of those mentioned, cellulose nitrate film is the most notorious. It should be copied onto a safety film and discarded from your holdings. Retention of this material in the repository is a serious fire hazard because it can burn without oxygen and degrades readily to produce combustible and poisonous gases. The other materials should also be copied for permanence by one of the many available methods, if possible. They can be kept in the collection, but should be isolated from adjacent material with sheets of polyester film or folders of alkaline-buffered paper. This will prevent degradation or staining of undamaged material. In addition, lignin-containing papers may be deacidified (the process by which damaging acid in the paper is neutralized and an alkaline earth carbonate is deposited in the paper fibers for future protection) as part of a professional treatment program to slow down degradation.

Damage often occurs during handling in spite of concern and good intentions. It may be a cumulative process or it may happen because an item is extremely fragile. Such damage can be avoided by restricting the handling. Consider special protection for these items. Popular items which are requested frequently will last longer when used by readers on microfilm or photocopy. This course is urged, except in special situations when it is necessary to consult the original. Vulnerable and valuable items should be given additional individual protection. Encapsulating unbound items in polyester film will eliminate wear and tear. Bound items and special-format items should have folded wrappers or special boxes.

3. *Know What You Have, Why You Have It, and What Value It Is to You*
    All of the written records associated with a historical item are important to its preservation. The knowledge of how you acquire an item, what its

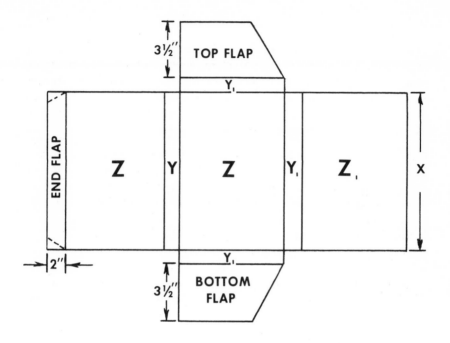

X = height of book + 1/8″
Y = maximum thickness of book + 3/32″
Y_1 = thickness of book + 1/16″
Z = width of book at widest part + 1/8″
Z_1 = width of book + 1/16″

The A.P.S. folder is made of a neutral, buffered folder stock (such as the Permatan handled by the Hollinger Corporation); the lightweight stock, 10 mil, is rigid enough to support a volume up to 3/8″ thick, the heavier weight, 20 mil, will support a volume (or pamphlet or set of leaves) up to 3″ thick. For example, the A.P.S. now uses these folders to store contemporary typescripts on 8½″ x 11″ paper.

To make the folders, only the folder stock, equipment consisting of a mat knife, calipers, ruler and square, and ample working surface are needed. A pair of sharp scissors can be substituted for the mat knife if necessary. The most important requirement is careful measurement according to the formula shown with the diagram; the fractional additions are allowances for the thickness of the stock as the case folds over on itself.

The folder was designed by Willman Spawn, conservator at the American Philosophical Society Library, in 1957 for the temporary storage of disbound pamphlets.

provenance is, and how it fits into the collection are important factors when planning a budget for conservation now and in the future. Items of importance to your collection may be insignificant to another institution. A professional conservator can tell you the extent and cost of the treatment required, but cannot tell you which items will be most valuable to your collection. Only the custodian guided by written records and familiar with the collection can establish preservation priorities which cover day-to-day handling as well as long-range planning and restoration.

4. *Keep Facilities Clean and Organized — Plan Regular Inspections*

This piece of advice seems almost too obvious to mention but far too important to omit. Good housekeeping and regular inspection can prevent serious damage from vermin or development of mold, and if insects or other pests do invade they are likely to be discovered before they can do real harm. When collections and work areas are clean and well organized, material is less likely to be misplaced, misidentified or inadvertently damaged.

In addition to inspection for cleanliness and general housekeeping, you should check regularly for collection condition, including books that need wrappers, acid folders that should be replaced, and any signs of unexpected deterioration or previously unnoticed damage. Keep a list of conditions which need to be corrected and mark the location in the storage area.

5. *Be Cautious About Exhibition*

One of the great custodial temptations is to display choice items from a collection. If you exercise restraint and weigh the pros and cons involved, exhibition can be a legitimate and satisfying function of your institution.

Exhibition is very hard on archival objects. Exposure to light damages them, and the extra handling involved in preparation for display is often harder on objects than ordinary use. Consider alternatives to permanent display for your treasures. There may be a low-value or expendable item which will create interest or illustrate the point you wish to make as well as an irreplaceable, valuable one. A good photograph of your most important item (with a caption explaining the preservation reasons why the original is not exhibited) can be very effective. Another possibility is to rotate display items frequently.

When you decide to exhibit original material, remember that a damaged item can never be completely restored to its initial condition. Each item also has a specific life in terms of exposure to light. Each time it is exhibited part of that life is used. Consider carefully the vulnerability, value and life expectancy before you make the decision.

Insist on safe display techniques when items are exhibited. All material should be prepared and supported for exhibition in non-damaging ways. This starts with careful handling of the item itself while it is being prepared. In addition, unbound paper items should be properly matted with alkaline mat board and exhibited under glass or ultraviolet-filtering UF-3 Plexiglas. Polyester encapsulation is an inexpensive alternative for permanent matting in many instances, but neither polyester nor plain glass filter ultraviolet light. Polyester is not suitable for pastel drawings, charcoals and other friable media. Bound books should be cradled so that their bindings are not strained.

All exhibited material should be protected from dust, ultraviolet light, relative humidity and temperature at variance with storage conditions, and from handling by visitors. Light sources should be outside, not inside any display case.

6. *Resist the Temptation to Repair Damaged Material Yourself*

Well-intentioned but inept repair treatment on valuable and irreplaceable items has done enormous damage. Pressure-sensitive mending tapes are notorious. The familiar yellow-brown stain from older tape is very difficult and sometimes even impossible to remove. Newer tapes can also cause problems, especially when the solvent required to move the adhesive also removes the image from the paper. Even repair with safe materials can be damaging or disfiguring when executed by an inexperienced person who misjudges the solubility of the ink or the response of a given paper to the repair technique. The cost of removing a tape stain or a bad mend is always greater than the cost of having a repair done correctly in the first place.

Bindings may often be important documentary evidence. Ill-considered restoration of rare or early books may cause more damage than leaving them untreated. Solutions designed to "restore" rotten crumbling leather should not be used. These solutions are often temporarily effective as a consolidant, but in time usually become stiff and brittle on the leather and cannot be satisfactorily removed. They tend to leave the surface of the leather with a shiny plastic appearance. A regular oiling program for leather bindings in good condition will be more beneficial to your collection than inappropriate restoration.

These are simple alternatives to do-it-yourself repairs which will prevent additional damage in most instances. When the pages of bound books have bad tears — which will get worse if they are not treated — use glassine stamp hinges. The adhesive is water soluble and does not discolor paper. If the hinges are applied sparingly, they can usually be removed by a conservator. For single sheets, polyester processing folders or polyester encapsulation will allow even brittle or torn material to be handled safely. Folded wrappers for bound books will keep the pieces together and prevent shelf damage until they can be rebound or restored.

7. *When You Don't Know or Are Uncertain, Ask for Help*

You will face situations and problems where the advice and assistance of a conservator will be invaluable. In addition to offering you guidance with a specific preservation problem, a professional conservator can provide a total restoration program for damaged items based on a survey of your collection. He will assess the present condition of your collection and project future conservation needs, as well as help with storage and environmental planning for a complete, balanced preservation program.

Many conservators and institutions employing conservators are happy to answer occasional telephone queries on a courtesy basis. In instances where they cannot answer your question, they will usually refer you to someone else. Do not expect to hear about actual treatment methods. In most cases careful examination is required before any course of treatment is planned.

For many small institutions concerned about preservation, one visit by a conservator can be an extremely useful investment. The information gained from the consultant's visit could be used to generate more funds for preservation and be the basis for a systematic long-term conservation/preservation program.

The American Institute for Conservation maintains a list of certified paper conservators and can provide assistance in finding conservators within a geographical area. This list can be obtained by writing to the American Institute for Conservation of Historic and Artistic Works, 1522 K Street N.W., Suite 804, Washington, D.C. 20005. Most large institutions with conservation facilities can either provide advice and answer questions or direct you to someone who can. The Preservation Office of the Library of Congress is always available to answer questions and has staff members with disaster experience.

As you consider the preceding guidelines and plan your strategy for preservation, remember that it is your daily efforts that are most important. You will be unable to do everything at once, or even in the first few months. The crucial thing is to be continually conscious of preservation and to keep at it. As your own program evolves you will acquire more specific knowledge and develop long-term goals. You may want to set up a program with a conservator or become involved in a cooperative conservation program with other institutions to get professional treatment designed especially for your collections. Your interest and concern will be contagious as others see the results. This awareness is ultimately your most important asset.

Bookbinding Needs
Of the Historical Society

By Jean Gunner

THE physical condition of many bound volumes is often worse in archival repositories than in circulating libraries. The poor condition of these bound materials usually stems from improper storage prior to their acquisition by the repository. Most materials are retrieved from damp basements or hot, dusty attics, often resulting in severe deterioration of the binding as well as the text block. Administrators of historical units and funding agencies, both federal and state, must be educated that allocation of time, space, personnel and money are necessary for the restoration and continuing care of the collection. Conditions for book collections are not static and such materials will deteriorate in time. No matter how small the institution and its operating budget, responsible curators must find some dollars for the conservation of the historical materials under their custody. An important objective is to work with your administrator in order to establish a commitment to conserve and preserve your collections.

Unfortunately, some administrators, curators and archivists in the past have assumed that since the materials have lasted as long as they have, there is no need for concern about the future. Much of the visible and invisible deterioration began in the industrial pollution of the nineteenth century. Pollutants such as sulfur dioxide will remain in the materials, some taking years to show harmful effects, while with others deterioration will be much more rapid. Even with the controlled atmosphere and filtered lighting that many collections now have, the rate of deterioration will only be retarded, because invisible chemical changes can be very damaging.

In order to deal with these problems efficiently, the collections should be surveyed and the materials grouped by stages of deterioration, e.g., severe, advanced, minimal and questionable. If this is not done, in time many materials will be beyond any form of restoration and will have to be either replaced or discarded.

The severe stage of deterioration should include those books that have brittle, crumbling pages, mold and insect infestation. To solve the two latter problems, investigate first of all the possibility of fumigation. Second, place the books into individual acid-free book boxes or wrap them in acid-free paper, and store flat. If fumigation is not possible, take the books outside and dust off the excess mold. Where mold is a continuing problem in an uncontrolled atmosphere, place saucers of Silica Gel crystals near the books. This will help to absorb excess humidity. When the crystals are saturated, they will change color. They can then be dried in an oven and used again several times. Where insects are a problem, try to identify the type. Natural history museums are usually very cooperative in this problem area. Then contact a local fumigation agency—many are listed in your local yellow pages—and seek correction for the problem, being sure that nothing used is harmful to the materials. (Yale University has adopted an interesting alternative to fumigation. It wraps its infested books individually in plastic and freezes them at -20° Fahrenheit for three days.)

The advanced group of deteriorating materials should include such problems as browning of the paper, detached boards and spines, loose pages, and leather red rot (powdery leather). Do not attempt to put leather dressing on books with red rot as you will end with a horrible, sticky mess. There is no cure for red rot, but if it is necessary to use such a book, make a dust jacket out of acid-free paper or non-plasticized polyester film. Spraying light coats of Krylon on powdering leather will help to consolidate it, but it must be handled with care. After spraying it, place it into individual boxes or wrap in acid-free paper and, if possible, store it flat.

The minimal group should include paper tears, loose hinges, dry leather and distorted bindings. The books with loose hinges and distorted bindings should be stored flat. The dry leather bindings should be treated first with potassium lactate solution, then with a mixture of sixty per cent neat's-foot oil and forty per cent anhydrous lanolin. (These items can be purchased from Talas, 104 Fifth Avenue, New York 10011, or The Bookbinder, 209 South Craig Street, Pittsburgh 15213.) Do not apply the dressing if the leather turns black while applying the potassium lactate. Great care should also be taken when applying the dressing so it does not damage the text block. All leather bindings should be treated this way every two to five years in order to keep the leather from becoming dry and brittle. Anything undetermined should be placed in the questionable group for evaluation at a later date.

Ideally, grants would be available to enable archivists to periodically bring in a conservator for an evaluation of the condition of the collection. If one is aware of the problems as well as a solution and has an idea of the costs involved, he or she is in a strong position to argue for action. A *Cultural Directory*, available from the Associated Councils of the Arts, Washington, D.C. (ISBN 0-915400-00-7), lists all the funding agencies and their services.

Until funding for restoration can be found, make the collection as "comfortable" as possible to retard further deterioration. Establish a program for keeping dust and dirt off the materials. Some institutions and libraries are now shelving by size—they have found that they end with more shelving space, plus the materials are much more "comfortable" this way. Remove loose papers and clippings from the books and house separately. Leaving things inside books can cause acid migration and distort the bindings. The temptation to "patch" torn pages and bindings in the desire to "do something" will often do more damage than good to the original material. Materials that have been "patched" often take two or three times longer to restore, so it is better to leave well enough alone. You should make yourself aware of the latest conservation methods. If you know what is reasonably possible, the visiting conservator will be able to spend more time on saving the collection rather than converting you.

Library schools should recognize the necessity of establishing a conservation course. Here the prospective librarian or archivist could teach the importance of environmental-control systems and learn restoration techniques so that he or she can preserve his or her collections. Half the battle is knowing what protective and restorative procedures can be taught and carried out by one's staff and what should be left to the professional. Individuals should also know how to distinguish a good restoration from a bad one.

Today, conservators are very open in sharing their practices and concepts with each other as well as those in charge of collections. We must work together to preserve the records of civilization.

Part 5

WHERE TO GO FOR HELP
State and Federal Sources

The Pennsylvania Historical And Museum Commission

By Harry E. Whipkey

THE Pennsylvania Historical and Museum Commission is the official historical agency for the Commonwealth of Pennsylvania. Included in its organizational structure are four major operational units: the Bureau of Museums, the Bureau of Historic Sites and Properties, the Office of Historic Preservation, and the Bureau of Archives and History. Each of these units has as a major objective the assistance and promotion, wherever possible, of responsible activities and programs of Pennsylvania's historical institutions, societies, agencies and related organizations and groups. In the area of archives and manuscripts, support to regional and local programs is provided by the Bureau of Archives and History and, more specifically, by that bureau's Division of Archives and Manuscripts (Pennsylvania State Archives).

The purpose of this paper is to discuss specific kinds of archival assistance available at the State Archives. At the outset, however, it might well be useful to explain briefly what the Historical and Museum Commission and its archival division are not in a position to do.

The Commission is not a grant-making agency. Its budget is restricted to meeting necessary expenses relevant to on-going programs as mandated by law. In fact, in order to meet established responsibilities in desirable ways, the Commission is itself constantly in quest of grant money and competes for public and private funds just as any other historical institution.

Given budget limitations and the related fact that there is currently a complement of only seven archivists to carry out the varied and complex assignments of the State Archives, it is not possible to assign a single professional to serve as a full-time field archivist, i.e., to be on immediate call to travel around the Commonwealth to provide direct, on-the-spot advice or supervision. This is not to say, as will be discussed later, that archivists are unable to visit local facilities or organizations if a special need exists or as other activities are scheduled in the locality.

In the area of microfilming, the photoduplication laboratory of the State Archives has limited capabilities and is on occasion able to provide services to regional and local repositories. But with only two planetary cameras, staff is generally hard pressed to keep pace with in-house microfilming projects and to meet the reference needs of research users at the

Archives search room. It is necessary to be selective, and to be realistic about capabilities.

However, if a major or emergency-type microfilming need develops, the Bureau would like to know about it. It would obviously do whatever it could, either placing the project into its own filming schedule or endeavoring to have the work done as economically as possible at some other responsible facility.

What Else Can the State Archives Do?

Individuals and small groups are invited to visit the State Archives, where one can receive a comprehensive tour and a detailed explanation of procedures and services at a major state archival agency. Located at the corner of Third and Forster streets in Harrisburg, the Archives complex includes staff offices and processing areas, a search room and a twenty-one-story records tower. All stack areas are air-conditioned, with controls for maintaining the proper temperature and humidity. This facility contains space for the storage of approximately one hundred fifteen thousand cubic feet of records.

The State Archives is open Monday through Friday, 8:30 to 4:45, except State legal holidays. Its holdings may be used by all responsible researchers who register at the search room, and who adhere to the stated regulations pertaining to the use of the records. Photocopying services (xerographic and photostatic copies, photographic prints, and microfilm) are available to facilitate the work of the researcher.

If it is possible for individuals to spend a day, part of a day, or several days at the Archives in Harrisburg, everything will be done to insure that the visit will be both interesting and informative. There visitors can study first hand how staff acquires, accessions and processes materials. The types of finding aids developed and the precautions taken in properly preserving historical items can also be observed. All that is asked is that trips to the State Archives be planned and scheduled in advance.

The archives staff considers it their responsibility to respond as quickly and as accurately as possible to telephone and mail inquiries which in any way relate to the care of archives and manuscripts. They can be contacted to answer questions on the proper disposition and preservation of endangered historical records located at the local level and to answer questions concerning the reference, processing or describing of records held in local repositories. Please place calls to the office of the director, Bureau of Archives and History (717-787-3051), or to the office of the Chief, Division of Archives and Manuscripts (717-787-2761). Letters should be addressed to the Bureau of Archives and History, Pennsylvania Historical and Museum Commission, Box 1026, Harrisburg 17120.

Pennsylvania State Archives Building

As noted above, the Division of Archives and Manuscripts is not in the position to provide the services of a full-time field archivist to travel around the Commonwealth, providing direct assistance. This certainly does not mean that it is incapable of providing support through visitations. In the event that a definite need exists, one requiring some on-the-spot consultation or help, the Archives will endeavor to free staff members from base responsibilities and send them to the respective facility. Depending on the circumstances, the bureau director might also contact the head of an established archival facility in the region and suggest the possibiity of some personal contact. Or those in need of advice or assistance might be informed of qualified individuals in the said area and subsequently initiate contacts themselves. In short, whatever seems most appropriate will be done.

In the event that an organization or institution is not equipped to adequately administer or house special types of archival or manuscript holdings, staff will gladly cooperate to find an appropriate home for such materials, be that home a college or university archives, a major county or regional historical society, the State Archives, or some other responsible repository. If historical materials are in need of fumigation, arrangements can be made to use the large machine in the Archives Building. Use of the fumigator chamber must be scheduled, however.

The Bureau of Archives and History will also work with individuals and repositories in providing information on grant programs. Up-to-date information on procedures and policies of grant-making agencies will be provided to prospective grantees by either forwarding available materials to them or by putting them in touch with appropriate individuals.

In matters involving grant possibilities through the National Historical Publications and Records Commission, states play a very large and direct role. William B. Fraley's paper, which follows, discusses the NHPRC's program in detail. But it should be pointed out here that the Historical and Museum Commission's Bureau of Archives and History administers the work of the State Historical Records Advisory Board in implementing the NHPRC's records grant activity in Pennsylvania. It provides detailed information on this federal commission's program, and it often reviews grant proposals prior to formal submission to the State Historical Records Advisory Board and the NHPRC.

The Bureau of Archives and History has prepared and the Historical and Museum Commission has published a booklet relating to historical organizations in Pennsylvania. In part, this booklet is a guide to funding sources for historical and related groups. It also details problems associated with running non-profit organizations.

The staff of the Bureau of Archives and History works closely with the officers and committees of the Pennsylvania Federation of Historical Societies in planning and conducting that organization's annual meetings and regional workshops. These are professional gatherings often featuring sessions relevant to the proper administration of archives and manuscripts. Staff also cooperates with the Pennsylvania Historical Association in arranging and staging the annual research conferences in Harrisburg. A major purpose of these conferences is to publicize the existence and availability of historical materials, located at historical societies, libraries, college and university archives, etc. across the Commonwealth, which relate to particular research needs or possibilities. Finally, news items concerning projects and important acquisitions of archival and manuscript repositories should be reported to the Bureau of Archives and History for possible placement in the Historical and Museum Commission's quarterly magazine, *Pennsylvania Heritage*.

The Public Committee for
The Humanities in Pennsylvania

By Gail Stern and William Schneider

THE Public Committee for the Humanities in Pennsylvania is a state-wide organization which awards grants for public outreach programs in the humanities. The committee itself is a private, volunteer citizens' group which receives most of its funds from the National Endowment for the Humanities in Washington, D.C. The committee retains a full-time staff to conduct its organizational operations and to implement its funding decisions.

Support is awarded on a competitive basis to non-profit organizations or groups in Pennsylvania — to colleges and universities, museums, libraries, historical societies, community groups and many others. The committee announces three deadlines a year for submitting proposals. Generally, funds are available for approved projects three months after the application deadlines. While grant size has varied tremendously (from a low of $1,000 to a high of $240,000), the average size of a committee grant is $10,000. As of April, 1979, more than 190 grants had been awarded in six years of operation, amounting to more than two and one-quarter million dollars.

The committee normally does not provide support for institutions on a sustaining basis, but does support a variety of humanities programs designed for public outreach. Most of the grants that have been made to archives, public libraries and historical organizations have supported the development of innovative programs for engaging the general public in activities related to the work of the institutions. Programs specifically designed for limited audiences, such as an organization's membership, are not eligible for support.

The humanities, as defined by Congress for the purposes of this program, include the study of philosophy, history, literature, jurisprudence, art history, ethics and other related fields. Humanists, usually defined as those who teach on the college level, write or otherwise work in some of the areas mentioned, are regularly involved in all stages of committee-funded projects. Humanists from nonacademic institutions, including historical societies and museums, have increasingly contributed their time and expertise as project directors and participants in committee-funded programs on numerous subjects — ranging from oral histories to interpretive exhibitions.

The majority of the committee's programs, during most of its five years of operation, brought together the general public and humanities scholars to discuss current issues of broad concern — including unemployment, educational policies, energy issues and societal images of the aging. The results of a comprehensive review and evaluation of the committee's grant-making program (undertaken between January, 1977, and June, 1978) led the committee to develop several new grant categories (an option extended by the 1976 Congressional legislation reauthorizing the NEH). Under the committee's "Special Program," *any* proposal which demonstrates a means of public outreach in the humanities is eligible for support.

While that description may seem pretty far removed from the day-to-day activities of archival or other historical organizations, there are clearly large areas for potential cooperation. At the risk of oversimplification, we can say that archival institutions are primarily interested in 1) gathering historical materials, 2) restoring and organizing them, and 3) making them available for use. In determining the kinds of support it could provide for libraries, archives and related institutions, the Public Committee has emphasized the third category of activity — the *use* of archival materials.

If a proposal to the committee calls for using materials that first must be collected or organized (or that have already been acquired but first must be put in usable form), some committee support may be provided to carry out the first two activities in order to accomplish the third. There is, of course, a question of degree; on the whole, the largest share of project budgets is used for the direct support of activities designed for outreach.

Some examples of past programs may help to illustrate the kinds of projects that might be considered eligible for support:

The Pennsylvania Ethnic Heritage Studies Center at the University of Pittsburgh received a committee grant to support outreach activities in cooperation with six neighborhood organizations. The purpose of the grant was "to raise the level of consciousness about historical records; — and to identify documents in the community and discuss the relevance of historical records to contemporary problems." A symposium was held in each neighborhood, featuring presentations by historians, archivists and others; a slide show illustrating research documents and related materials from each community; and a period for open discussion. The programs were very successful in generating further activities in each community; in almost every neighborhood the audience eagerly undertook follow-up projects in cooperation with archives, by offering to aid in the collection of materials or by using collected materials to help produce local histories.

Temple University's Urban Archives Center in Philadelphia received a grant to do a program based to some extent on the PEHSC model. Like the Pittsburgh program, the Urban Archives Center plans to work directly with neighborhood groups. But in this project, funds will support the active involvement of the neighborhood residents in direct use of the resources of the archives and other institutions, and in the gathering of new resources. Each neighborhood group will document some aspect of its history with the assistance of humanists and a community coordinator. The groups will determine their own strategies for documentation — through photographs, oral history interviews or primary source materials. A concluding workshop will assess the results of the neighborhood projects and discuss the preservation, disposition and maintenance of the materials created or discovered in the course of the project.

Another project, entitled "Bilingual Community Access to Ethnic Cultural Resources," consisted of four discussion programs sponsored by Taller Puertorriqueno (The Puerto Rican Workshop) in Philadelphia. The programs (panel presentations followed by discussion), were all bilingual, and centered around access to cultural resources, including published educational materials and cultural artifacts, and access to tools for community self-study (such as oral history and photography).

The programs described above are meant to serve only as examples of projects that might be undertaken by archives or other historical institutions in an effort to broadly serve the public through the use of their resources. The "Special Program" grant category offers an ideal opportunity for sponsors who wish to develop other kinds of innovative outreach programs. In addition to an ongoing "Humanities and Contemporary Issues Program" and the "Special Program," the committee has instituted three other funding categories: a Media Program, a Fellowship Program and a Planning Grant Program. In addition, an Arts/Humanities funding program has been instituted in cooperation with the Pennsylvania Council on the Arts.

Applications for amounts up to $15,000 are considered eligible for "outright" support by the committee and carry a matching requirement which can be met by cash or in-kind contributions from the project sponsors or other groups or individuals affiliated with the project. In-kind contributions include time donated by project participants or staff, donated meeting facilities, or other contributions. For funding requests over $15,000, "Gift-and-Matching" support is available. This type of support requires that applicants secure gifts from non-federal donor(s), such as corporations, foundations or state or local funding sources. These gifts, which are matched in varying proportions by the federal treasury, return additional federal dollars to Pennsylvania over and above the committee's established level of NEH support.

The Committee staff regularly advises applicants in the preparation of proposals, and may be contacted, for more information or application materials, at The Public Committee for the Humanities in Pennsylvania, 401 North Broad Street, Suite 818, Philadelphia 19108, telephone (215) 925-1004 or 1005.

The National Endowment
For the Humanities

By Jeffrey Field

THE National Endowment for the Humanities is an independent federal grant-making agency created by Congress in 1965 to support projects of research, education and public activity in the humanities. According to the Act which established the Endowment, the humanities include, but are not limited to, the following fields: history, philosophy, languages, literature, linguistics, archeology, jurisprudence, history and criticism of the arts, ethics, comparative religion, and those aspects of the social sciences employing historical or philosophical approaches.

The Endowment's operations are conducted through divisions which administer most of its programs. The Division of Research Grants provides support for group projects of research in the humanities, for research collections, for the preparation of important research tools, and for the editing of important humanistic texts. It is through the division's Research Collections Program that support for archival projects is provided.

The Research Collections Program

The purpose of the Research Collections Program is to make the raw materials of research more accessible to scholars. The program helps develop collections by microfilming materials in foreign repositories so that they will be available in the United States, and by limited use of oral history techniques to collect data. It increases access to materials through support of projects which address national problems in the archival and library field, through pilot projects in systems development and library bibliographic networking, and through grants to catalog, inventory or otherwise gain bibliographic control of significant research collections, both print and non-print. It is this third type of project which is supported most often by the collections program.

All applications submitted to the collections program are examined by eight to twelve individual reviewers, including scholars who are specialists in the subject area of the proposal and archivists or special collections librarians. Following individual review, applications are presented as a group to a panel of five or six archivists and librarians, who provide a comparative evaluation of all applications in the group. The assessments of specialist reviewers and panelists are presented to the National Council on the Humanities. The council recommends applications for the approval of the Endowment's chairman, who has final grant-making authority.

Grant Applications

The basic criteria used to determine whether or not a particular application for a collections grant warrants funding include the potential research use of the collection by advanced scholars in the humanities, the immediacy of the need to make the materials accessible, the professionalism of the staff, and the soundness of the work plan.

Applications should discuss the extent to which the collection is a unique resource for scholarship. If an institution lacks the staff expertise to evaluate a collection adequately, it should consider bringing in a consultant to provide such a description before submitting an application to process the collection. The collections program offers a limited number of grants for institutions to employ a consultant to examine collections and provide advice on the methodology most appropriate for making them accessible.

Successful applications are those that have made a clear case for the research value of the collection and have provided specific technical details regarding the size of the collection, in linear or cubic feet (or number of titles if the materials are published); the methodology for processing, with examples of the product such as sample entries, cards, print-outs, registers or inventories; the functions assigned to all personnel; an estimated rate of progress in man-hours; the stages in which completion of the project is to be achieved; and a description of the product at the end of each stage. Projects may be planned for a duration of three years. Applicant institutions are expected to bear approximately forty per cent of total project costs.

Collections that are already accessible to scholars, even though their indices or catalogs are less than ideal, do not usually form the basis of a competitive application. Oral history which is not an integral part of a collection of other types of research materials will not be eligible in the program. It is important, therefore, to relate an oral history project closely to its archival base and describe how it will fill gaps in an existing collection. The collections program does not make grants for acquisitions or for operating costs, nor can it provide funds for the organization of collections of modern records generated by units of federal, state and local governments; for records management projects in general; or for contemporary collections of congressional papers or the papers of other public officials.

Collections program staff are available for consultation with potential applicants. Staff suggest that initial inquiries be made through a brief letter describing a project idea. Staff will comment upon the eligibility of the project and provide potential applicants with application instructions and program guidelines.

Institutions are encouraged to submit a detailed, preliminary-draft application for further staff review well in advance of the application deadlines. For additional information on the program guidelines and proposal deadlines, correspondence should be addressed to Research Collections, Mail Stop 350, National Endowment for the Humanities, Washington, D.C. 20506.

The National Historical Publications And Records Commission

By William Fraley

FEDERAL assistance for archival and archives-related projects is available from two principal sources. The two programs are the Research Collections Program of the National Endowment for the Humanities (NEH) and the Historical Records Program of the National Historical Publications and Records Commission (NHPRC). The purpose of this paper, which will focus on the second of these two federal funding agencies, is to familiarize potential applicants with the Records Program and to explain how it might fit the particular needs of individual historical societies and archival units.

The Historical Records Program of the NHPRC is designed to encourage greater efforts by state and local governments and by private institutions and organizations to preserve and make available for use records that further an understanding and appreciation of American history. This encouragement takes the form of grants in support of a variety of projects which fall within the following categories:

1. Survey and accessioning projects—more specifically, projects concerned with locating, identifying and evaluating historical records, and planning or arranging for their transfer to appropriate repositories.

2. Preservation and reproduction projects—projects concerned primarily with the physical condition of records. This category includes preservation of the informational content of historical records by microform reproduction.

3. Records use projects—projects designed to facilitate the use of records by researchers and to improve the ability of repositories to provide adequate reference service.

4. Archival techniques projects—projects whose principal objective is the development or discussion of techniques and practical skills related to the preservation and use of records.

5. Feasibility projects—projects to determine the feasibility of undertaking more extensive or more comprehensive projects in any of the above categories. This category includes providing for consultants to advise on appropriate methodology and techniques.

Although the NHPRC is ultimately responsible for determining which projects receive funding, it is assisted in making its decisions by Historical Records Advisory Boards in the various states. These advisory boards are composed of professional archivists, manuscript curators, historians and others knowledgeable in the administration and use of historical records. Each advisory board, whose members are appointed by the governor, is chaired by a state historical records coordinator, also appointed by the governor pursuant to criteria established by the NHPRC. The advisory boards review all records proposals submitted from their respective states, except those whose activities transcend state boundaries, and make advisory recommendations to the NHPRC regarding funding. In addition, the Advisory Boards are charged with the responsibility of determining the needs of their respective states with regard to records preservation and accessibility, with a view toward devising effective ways to meet those needs.

It should be apparent then that the NEH and the NHPRC consider and may support a number of similar activities. There are, however, a number of features about the two programs which distinguish one from the other and may bear upon an applicant's choice of which program to approach for grant support. Some of these distinguishing features follow:

1. Subject Matter: The NHPRC confines its support to projects relating to historical records which may be important to an understanding and appreciation of the history of the United States. It does not support projects relating to records from other countries, unless such materials relate directly to American history in some way. The NEH, on the other hand, is not restricted either to American history or to documentary materials.

2. Types of Materials: The NHPRC may support projects involving records regardless of medium, including photographs, film, audio recordings, etc. It does not, however, presently support projects relating to newspapers, rare books or other published materials, except where these are part of a manuscript or archival collection. The NHPRC also does not currently support oral history interviewing or transcribing, although it will consider projects to preserve existing oral history tapes or transcripts.

The NEH's support extends not only to institutions holding historical records, but also to those with special research collections, including artifacts. The NEH, however, does not currently support projects relating to records created by state or local governments, whereas the NHPRC does.

3. Allowable Costs: Records proposals submitted to the NHPRC may include requests to fund the cost of publication of finding aids, manuals, and other project materials. The NEH cannot provide funds for actual publication. The NHPRC will consider requests for support for the full range of records conservation and preservation activities, although its primary concern is with preservation of the informational content of historical records, and not with the records' artifact value; therefore, special

emphasis is placed on microform reproduction for preservation purposes. While the NEH will, occasionally, provide funds for basic preservation activities, it prefers that such work be contributed as cost sharing. Neither program will provide funds to pay for duplicating materials already accessible in the United States in order to create a collection.

The NEH will provide limited funds for equipment rental or purchase. The NHPRC will support equipment purchase or rental only in exceptional circumstances. Both programs require substantial institutional cost sharing for supported projects. The NEH requires at least forty per cent, whereas the NHPRC does not set a definite level. The NEH will fund a portion of an applicant's indirect project costs, provided the applicant has a negotiated indirect cost rate with a federal agency. The NHPRC, because of its limited funding, does not normally support indirect costs, although an applicant may include such costs as part of its cost sharing. Both programs give preference to grants which can be made on a matching basis. Matching requirements differ, however, and applicants are advised to consult program literature regarding the respective requirements.

4. Review Procedures and Funding Cycles: Proposals are submitted directly to the NEH currently against an annual deadline. The proposals go through several review stages, and funding recommendations are made by the National Council on the Humanities to the chairman of the National Endowment, who alone has the authority to approve funding. The minimum time between submission and notification that a grant is being made is approximately six months.

The NHPRC meets three times a year and deadlines for submission of proposals to be considered at each meeting are set several months in advance of the meeting dates. All state proposals are submitted through the appropriate State Historical Records Advisory Board. Following review by the Advisory Board, the proposals are forwarded to the NHPRC staff for presentation to the commission. Regional and national proposals—proposals whose activities transcend state boundaries—are submitted directly to the NHPRC staff. The minimum time from submission to notification of NHPRC action is approximately five months.

Prospective applicants are encouraged to discuss their particular needs with the respective program staffs. Submission of draft proposals for preliminary comment and suggestions is also encouraged. For additional information about the programs, write Research Collections Program, Division of Research Grants, Mail Stop 350, National Endowment for the Humanities, Washington, D.C. 20506, or Records Program, National Historical Publications and Records Commission, National Archives Building, Washington 20408.

Appendix I

Sample DEED of GIFT

We, the Corporation for the Relief of Widows and Orphans of Clergymen of the Protestant Episcopal Church in the Commonwealth of Pennsylvania, give to the Historical Society of Pennsylvania, for the general use of the Society, the materials described below:

Minutes, 1769-1931, 4 vols.

Minutes of the Acting Committee, 1903-15.

Manuscript correspondence of Bp. White and others concerning the management of the Corporation, 1760s-1890s (c. 150 pieces).

Ms. Table of Premiums, n.d.

Charter of the Corporation, parchment, enrolled 1771

Charter of the Corporation, paper, enrolled 1813

Samples of Endowment Policies: #2, #6, #8, #43, #48, #78, #122, #143, #183, #196, #218, #245, #254, #261, #319, #326, #661, #893, #1107, #1399.

Blotters, 1878-94, 2 vols.

Cash Books, 1894-1941, 7 vols.

Mortgage Book, 1930-48

21 volumes of Constitution, By-Laws and Histories of the Corporation.

The collection will be known as the "Records of the Corporation for the Relief of Widows and Orphans of Clergymen of the Protestant Episcopal Church."

We understand that these materials will be made available to researchers subject only to the Society's usual practices in granting access to research materials. We understand, too, that officers of and persons authorized by the Widow's Corporation will have unlimited access to the above materials for use in the Historical Society of Pennsylvania.

We understand that we have donated and conveyed to the Historical Society of Pennsylvania whatever rights, including literary rights, that we may have had in this material. Researchers may cite, edit, or publish any of these materials without our permission.

We further understand that some of these materials may duplicate those already owned by the Historical Society of Pennsylvania or may be judged as not pertinent to the collection by the Society's professional staff; the Society may exchange, sell, or dispose of unwanted materials should we not wish to have them returned.

We do/do not wish to have unwanted materials returned.

Date: _____

_____
(for the Corporation)

Accepted for the Historical Society of Pennsylvania

Sample Deposit Agreement

The Historical Society of Pennsylvania

This Historical Society of Pennsylvania offers to act as the archival repository for the Glen Mills School under the following terms and conditions:

1. The Historical Society of Pennsylvania will initially offer storage space for the School's valuable records for a term of ten years at no charge, until such time as funds are found to process the materials in proper archival fashion. During this initial period the collections would be unavailable to any but authorized representatives or the School of the professional staff of the Historical Society of Pennsylvania.

2. The Historical Society of Pennsylvania agrees to join with the School in seeking funding for the archival processing and description of the materials. Such processing and description will include, but not necessarily be limited to:

    a. Sorting and arranging the School's records by function (*i.e.*, administration, financial, pupil personnel, etc.);

    b. Housing the record groups in proper, acid-free folders and boxes;

    c. Preparing an unpublished description of the record groups for use in the Historical Society of Pennsylvania and by the School;

    d. Preparing a microfilm of the record groups for deposit at the School and for use at the Historical Society of Pennsylvania;

    e. Reporting the deposit to the National Union Catalogue of Manuscript Collections.

It is anticipated that the above objectives could be accomplished at a cost of $15,000 in one year; a, b, c and e alone would cost about $8,000.

3. The Historical Society of Pennsylvania further agrees to abide by the access restrictions imposed by the School. The Historical Society of Pennsylvania suggests that these restrictions be as follows:

a. The Historical Society of Pennsylvania will be empowered by the school to judge who has a legitimate need to use the materials. In so doing, we will only be extending to the School's records the criteria that we apply to our own.

b. The Historical Society of Pennsylvania will apply a "rolling" restriction of perhaps thirty years to administrative and financial records and fifty years to pupil personnel files.

c. The Historical Society of Pennsylvania will send a copy of the application of each researcher granted access to the School's records to the School.

4. The agreement is to be reviewed at the tenth anniversary of signing and may be terminated by either the School or the Society without prejudice upon sixty days' written notice after the tenth anniversary. It is understood that the archives remain the property of the Glen Mills School.

Appendix II

Representative rules for use of collections at

The Historical Society of Pennsylvania

Information about the nature and extent of the manuscript collections of the Society is to be found in *Guide to the Manuscript Collections of The Historical Society of Pennsylvania,* Second Edition (Philadelphia, 1949), and in *The National Union Catalog of Manuscript Collections.* The collections are for research work by qualified and experienced persons, and not for undergraduate study, prize competition, genealogical, or secondary school work.

Hours: Monday, 1 p.m. to 9 p.m.; Tuesday through Friday, 9 a.m. to 5 p.m. Closed Saturday, Sunday, and Certain Holidays.

RULES FOR USE

1. A card of admission for use of these collections may be requested by making written application to the office of the Director or the Chief of the Manuscript Department. Each applicant shall be required to show acceptable identification, and to supply the name and address of a person who can verify the statements made on the application. Graduate students may be asked to produce letters of introduction and recommendation from their advisors. Cards of admission are not transferable and are granted for specific subjects and limited periods.

2. A separate request or call slip, clearly written, and with all required information supplied, must be submitted for each volume, piece, or series desired. Materials will not be paged before 12:00 M. (5:00 P.M. Mondays) or after 4:30 P.M. (8:30 P.M. Mondays), unless call slips have been submitted the previous day. First-day users are excepted.

3. No manuscript, map, or print may be removed from the search room of the Manuscript Department to any other part of the building. All must be handled with extreme care and delicacy. All materials must be kept flat on the tops of reading tables.

4. Manuscripts may be consulted only by the reader signing for them, and may not be transferred to other readers.

5. Readers must not use fountain pens for taking notes, must not mark in any way, write upon, or lean upon manuscripts, maps, and prints produced for their use. The existing order and arrangement of unbound materials must be preserved, and any disarrangement must be reported to the attendants. No tracings or rubbings may be made.

6. Permission for the use of typewriters, tape recorders, or other reproducing equipment must be obtained from the Chief of the Manuscript Department.

7. Copies of materials under the care of the Manuscript Department may be obtained under such terms and conditions established by the Society and subject to the doctrine of "Fair Use" as defined by the Copyright Statute of 1976. Copies made by microfilming, xerography or photography are for reference purposes only; they may not be copied or reproduced in any way without the written permission of the Director of the Society.

8. Permission to publish, reproduce, reprint or quote from materials in the Society's collections must be secured in writing from the Director. The Historical Society of Pennsylvania does not surrender any rights in the material when permission for reproduction is given. The Society assumes no responsibility for copyright infringement or violation. It is the responsibility of the prospective user or his publisher to obtain the required permissions for the clearance of literary rights. Use of certain materials MAY be subject to a reproduction fee.

9. All persons permitted to use the manuscripts are required to sign the Department's register on each visit.

10. Readers are requested to leave all materials on the tables. Items to be reserved should be clearly marked with the date of future use.

Date . . . .

I have read the foregoing rules of the Historical Society of Pennsylvania and agree to abide by their provisions. Accordingly, I hereby apply for a card of admission to the Manuscript Department.

Signature in full . . . .

Name (please print). . . . .

Local Address. . . . . Telephone. . . . .

Permanent Address . . . .

. . . . Telephone . . . .

Profession . . . . Institution . . . .

PURPOSE OF STUDY

1. *Research for a Degree*   2. *Research for Publication*

   Degree . . . .   (   ) Book

   Professor . . . .   (   ) Other

   Subject . . . .   Subject . . . .

   . . . .

   . . . .

3. *Purpose, other than 1 or 2* . . . .

   . . . .

   . . . .

4. *Published Works by Applicant*

   Title . . . .   Title . . . .

   Publisher . . . .   Publisher . . . .

5. *Libraries in Vicinity Already Consulted*

   . . . .

   . . . .

6. *Reference*

   Name . . . .

   Address . . . .

Appendix III

Terminology for common photographic and print processes
Photography
I. Processes (use photoprint as a general term)
   A. Black and white (may be sepia-toned, gold-toned, etc.; may be a type, e.g., *carte-de-visite,* cabinet card, etc.)
       1. Albumen photoprint
       2. Ambrotype
       3. Black and white transparency
       4. Bromoil photoprint
       5. Calotype (Talbotype)
       6. Cyanotype (Blue print)
       7. Daguerreotype
       8. Emulsion-paper photoprint
       9. Gelatin silver photoprint
      10. Gum bichromate photoprint
      11. Palladium photoprint
      12. Photogravure
      13. Platinum photoprint
      14. Salted paper photoprint
      15. Stereograph (half or full)
         a. Daguerreotype stereograph
         b. Glass stereograph
         c. Card stereograph
         (d. Lithoprint stereograph — non-photographic)
      16. Tintype
      17. Woodburytype
   B. Color
       1. Carbo color photoprint
       2. Cibachrome photoprint (commercial name)
       3. Color photoprint
       4. Color transparency (by size)
       5. Dye transfer photoprint
   C. Photomechanical reproduction
       1. Collotype
       2. Half-tone reproduction
       3. Photogravure (reproduction)

II. Photo-negatives (color or black and white)
  A. Film photo-negative
  B. Glass photo-negative

Original print processes

   1. Aquatint
     Sugar lift aquatint (lift ground aquatint)
   2. Collograph
   3. Drypoint
   4. Engraving
     a. Copper engraving
     b. Line engraving
     c. Steel engraving
     d. Stipple engraving
   5. Etching
     Soft ground etching
   6. (Inkless) embossed print
   7. Intaglio
   8. Letterpress
   9. Linoleum cut (linocut)
  10. Linoleum engraving
  11. Lithograph
     Chromolithograph
  12. Metal cut
  13. Mezzotint
  14. Mixed media print
  15. Monotype
  16. Niello print
  17. Offset
  18. Photolithograph
  19. Photo silkscreen
  20. Relief print
  21. Silkscreen (serigraph)
  22. Woodcut
     Chiaroscuro woodcut
  23. Wood engraving

Appendix IV

A Security Checklist for Repositories

A. The Exterior Perimeter

_____ Define it. Is the archives a separate building? Rooms in building? City attached building? Etc.?

_____ Who has responsibility for perimeter security? (May not be the archives if it is located in another building.)

_____ What is the perimeter constructed of? Masonry? Plaster and lath? Etc.? (Has bearing on fire security.)

_____ Examine the perimeter and the area around it. Outside, are there weeds, shrubs, trees, etc., that would allow someone to hide close to the building? Is there exterior lighting, and is it secure? Is there access to the roof? Basement? Inside, examine the halls and walls around the archives for weak points.

_____ Openings: Are they all necessary? Are doors sturdy and in good condition? Do doors have glass panels near their locks? Are door hinges heavy-duty with non-removable screws and non-removable hinge pins? How many windows are there that are accessible from the ground? Do these windows have locks? What type are they? (Standard thumb latches are virtually worthless.) Do they have protective grills or roll-down shutters? Is there break-resistant glass or plastic in these windows? Are upper-level windows accessible from roofs, fire escapes, trees, adjacent buildings, etc.? What locks are installed on such windows? Are there other openings in the perimeter such as air conditioning piping, heating-plumbing tunnels, etc.? Are they protected with grills, etc.?

_____ Control of openings: Who carries keys to the door locks? Do all these persons need to have keys? How often are the locks routinely rekeyed? Are locks rekeyed when a key is lost? Or when a key-carrying staff member leaves the staff? Are there electronic alarms protecting the doors? Windows? If so, where is the alarm sounded during public hours? After hours? Who responds to the alarms? Is the wiring of the alarm system so protected that it cannot easily be cut or tampered with? Are there security guards? Who employs them, the archives or the parent institution?

_____ What is your assessment of the perimeter security?

B. Interior Perimeters

_____ What areas of the archives are public, and which are limited to the
staff only? Do the restricted areas require the use of a special key
for access? If so, who carries these keys? Do they all need them? Are
the special keys carried out of the archives at night? Why? Is there
an area of special security, such as a vault? If so, who has the combination, and do they all need to have it? Is the combination written down anyplace? Why? How often is the combination changed
routinely? Is it changed when a staff member who knows the combination leaves the staff? Who has access to the vault other than
those who have the combination? Is there electronic security on any
of the interior perimeters? Who monitors it during and after public
hours? Who responds to the alarms?

_____ What is your assessment of the interior security perimeters? Could
they be improved? If so, how?

C. Internal Security

_____ What sort of internal security exists? Is there a security officer?
What authority does he/she have? What assistants? Is there a guard
force? To whom do the guards report?

_____ Staff: How are prospective staff members screened before employment? Are credentials checked? Are employees bonded for surety as
well as performance? Are employees required to submit brief cases,
purses, etc., for inspection before leaving the building? Are
members of the staff allowed in the archives at other than regular
working hours? What records of such activity are kept? Whose
permission is required? Are the employees allowed to collect
materials in the same fields in which the institution collects? To
publish in these areas? Are the employees conscious of and
interested in security and its associated problems? Are training
programs in security offered to staff on a regular basis to increase
their knowledge?

_____ Non-Staff: Do any persons other than staff have access to security
areas of the building? Why? Who approves such access, and what
records are kept? Can permission for access be withdrawn if
abused?

_____ What is your assessment of the internal security? Could it be improved? If so, how?

D. Movement of Collections in the Archives

_____ What is the procedure for moving a collection in the building when needed by a patron or a staff member? Are dummies used to replace boxes and/or documents that are withdrawn from their filing locations? Is the filing location recorded and kept with the boxes and/or documents to speed refiling? Who locates the material needed and moves it? Does the material leave a security area during movement? Who reshelves the boxes and/or documents after use? What records are kept of such use? Are call slips used by patrons to request materials? By staff? Are the call slips retained permanently (they can assist in proving ownership)? How are the slips filed if they are kept?

_____ What is your assessment of the procedure used for the movement of collections in the archives? Could it be improved? If so, how?

E. Photocopying Procedure

_____ Who makes the photocopies requested by the patrons? If staff, is it archives staff, or institutional staff? If copies must be made by someone outside the archives (or the institution), what security procedure is followed? Does material leave the premises of the archives or the institution? What procedure is followed by patrons who wish to purchase photocopies? If material is pulled from a collection for photocopying, what control system is used? Who refiles such material? What records are kept of materials copied (can be used to provide proof of ownership)?

_____ What is your assessment of the photocopying procedure? Could it be improved? If so, how?

F. Reading Room Security

_____ Physical layout: What is the physical layout? Draw a plan of it. Can the staff keep a close watch on all the research tables? Can researchers move directly to the tables upon entering the room, or is there a barrier? Can a researcher already registered and seated at a table be approached by someone not registered so that something might be handed to the latter? Where are the reference books, registers, card catalogs, etc.? Does the staff member on duty have to move to this area to assist patrons? If so, can he/she still view all of the research tables? Where are the microform readers? Is a staff member assisting a patron with their use still able to view all the research tables? How many doors to the reading room are there? Are they locked or unlocked during public hours? If unlocked, do they pose a risk if an unauthorized person slips through? Are all exits and windows visible from the staff control desk?

_____ Where is the entrance to the stacks? Is it visible to patrons? Is it kept locked? If so, who has the keys? Are the keys always carried by staff members, or are they kept where a patron might obtain access after observing the staff?

_____ How is material brought to the reading room? Who brings it? Is the reading room ever left unattended while collections are brought to the patrons? If so, why?

_____ Who supervises the reading room? How many persons are assigned to the reading room staff? Do staff members have other work to perform while working in the reading room? Is the reading room supervised at all times when patrons are present? Are there security guards in addition to the archives staff? Do the guards have police powers? What are the guards' duties? Do reading room staff have any special training in security procedures? Is there a written procedure for the reading room staff to follow if they observe a patron concealing something? If they observe a patron carrying archives material out the door of the reading room?

_____ Researchers: What screening process is used when they first arrive? Must they fill out a registration form? Must identification be shown at the time of registration? Is it checked? How? Are patrons permitted to take their brief cases, purses, personal books, etc., into the research area? Why? Are researchers required to submit personal belongings for inspection by staff members before they leave the reading room? If not, why not? Can patrons be physically searched? if so, are they properly warned of this possibility by signs, notice in the registration form, etc.? If not, why not?

_____ Collection Use: How does a researcher obtain the material he wishes to see? Are there collection request forms or slips? How much material is a researcher allowed to have at a table at one time? Are boxes and folders checked after a researcher is finished with them? Are they checked before material is handed to a researcher? If a researcher may have only one or two boxes at a table, but a truckload of boxes is brought from the stacks to speed his work, where are the extra boxes kept until needed? Can researchers gain access to the material on the trucks, or in the temporary storage area? *See also*: Photocopying Procedure above.

_____ What is your assessment of the reading room security? Could it be improved? If so, how?

G. Security and the Law

_____ Are staff members working in the reading room thoroughly familiar with the laws governing the mutilation or theft of archival materials? Is concealment of material a crime in your jurisdiction? What do reading room personnel do if they should observe someone concealing something under clothing? What do they do if they merely suspect someone has concealed something? Do reading room staff have any protection from prosecution if they mistakenly but honestly accuse a patron of having concealed archival material? Do staff members have the authority to detain someone they suspect? Have the local police authorities been invited to inspect the reading room and discuss with the staff the problems of dealing with a thief, or with a suspected thief? Has an attorney been consulted about the laws of the jurisdiction that might apply in such situations?

H. Other Aspects of Security

_____ Do catalogs, calendars, complete and accurate accession records, security copies, shelf lists, etc., exist that will provide data for the police and other agencies if archival materials are stolen, and that will assist in proving ownership of the materials in court should a case be brought to trial? Are documents in the collection stamped or otherwise marked to show ownership by the archives?
_____ Are regular inventories of the holdings, or at least of the most valuable materials (such as those in the vault) conducted regularly?
_____ Is there an insurance policy with a schedule (detailed description of each item insured) of the items covered by the policy?
_____ Has the local law-enforcement agency been invited to inspect the archives to provide security recommendations, and to discuss security problems with the staff?
_____ What is your assessment of these aspects of the archives' security program? Could they be improved? How?

I. Fire Security

_____ Are fire extinguishers available in all areas of the archives? Have staff members been trained to use them? Have they seen demonstrations of their use and practiced with them? What types of extinguishers are available? Are the staff aware of the uses of each type?
_____ Are fire-extinguishing systems such as CO_2, Halon, or sprinklers, etc., available? Does the system have an alarm that is set off when it

goes into action? Where does the alarm sound, and who responds to it? Has the fire-extinguishing system (and the alarm, if present) been tested recently?

_____ Is there a smoke and/or heat-detection system? Where does it sound its alarm? Does it sound during public hours? After hours? Who responds to its signals? Has it been tested lately?

_____ Is there a staff-training program of what to do in case of fire? Are written procedures available describing what the staff should do in case of fire. Are there evacuation plans for staff and patrons? What security measures are taken to protect the materials in the archives during a fire emergency (the fire might be a diversion to allow someone to get into the stacks)?

_____ Has the local fire department been invited to inspect the premises? If so, did it make recommendations, and were they carried out? Why not?

_____ What is your assessment of the fire-security program in the archives? Could fire security be improved? If so, how?

Select Bibliography

General Works:

BORDIN, RUTH B., and WARNER, ROBERT M. *The Modern Manuscript Library.* New York and London: The Scarecrow Press, 1966.

DUCKETT, KENNETH W. *Modern Manuscripts: A Practical Manual for Their Management, Care and Use.* Nashville: American Association for State and Local History, 1975.

EVANS, FRANK B. *Modern Archives and Manuscripts: A Select Bibliography.* Chicago: Society of American Archivists, 1975.

———. "Modern Concepts of Archives Administration and Records Management," *Unesco Bulletin for Libraries,* XXIV (September/October, 1970), 242-47.

EVANS, FRANK B., *et al.* "A Basic Glossary for Archivists, Manuscript Writers and Records Managers," *American Archivist,* XXXVII (July, 1974), 415-33. (Also available as a reprint from the Society of American Archivists, Chicago.)

JENKINSON, HILARY. *A Manual of Archive Administration.* Edited by Roger H. Ellis. 2d rev. ed. London: Percy Lund, Humphries and Co., 1965.

JONES, H. G. *The Records of a Nation: Their Management, Preservation, and Use.* New York: Atheneum, 1969.

KANE, LUCILLE M. *A Guide to the Care and Administration of Manuscripts.* 2d ed. Nashville: American Association for State and Local History, 1961.

SCHELLENBERG, THEODORE R. *The Management of Archives.* New York: Columbia University Press, 1965.

Archival Methodology:

Appraisal and Accessioning

BRICHFORD, MAYNARD J. *Archives and Manuscripts: Appraisal and Accessioning.* ("Society of American Archivists Basic Manual Series.") Chicago, 1977.

BROOKS, PHILIP C. "The Selection of Records for Preservation," *American Archivist,* III (October, 1940), 221-34.

DOLLAR, CHARLES M. "Appraising Machine-Readable Records," *American Archivist,* XLI (October, 1978), 423-30.

KALENSKI, GUSTAVE. "Record Selection," *American Archivist,* XXXIX (January, 1976), 25-43.

LEWINSON, PAUL. "Archival Sampling," *American Archivist,* XX (October, 1957), 291-312.

PINKETT, HAROLD T. "Accessioning Public Records: Anglo-American Practices and Possible Improvements," *American Archivist,* XLI (October, 1978), 413-21.

———. "Identification of Records of Continuing Value," *Indian Archives,* XVI (January, 1965/December, 1966), 54-61.

———. "Selective Preservation of General Correspondence," *American Archivist,* XXX (January, 1967), 33-43.

Arrangement and Description

BERNER, RICHARD C. "Manuscripts Collections and Archives—A Unitary Approach," *Library Resources and Technical Services,* IX (Spring, 1965), 213-20.

BRUBAKER, ROBERT L. "Archival Principles and the Curator of Manuscripts," *American Archivist,* XXIX (October, 1966), 505-14.

EVANS, FRANK B. "Modern Methods of Arrangement of Archives in the United States," *American Archivist*, XXIX (April, 1966), 241-63.

GORDON, ROBERT S. "Suggestions for Organization and Description of Archival Holdings of Local Historical Societies." *American Archivist*, XXVI (January, 1963), 19-39.

GRACY, DAVID B., II. *Archives and Manuscripts: Arrangement and Description.* ("Society of American Archivists Basic Manual Series.") Chicago, 1977.

HAMER, PHILIP M. "Finding Mediums in the National Archives: An Appraisal of Six Years' Experience," *American Archivist*, V (April, 1952), 82-92.

SOCIETY OF AMERICAN ARCHIVISTS. *Inventories and Registers: A Handbook of Techniques and Examples.* Chicago: SAA, 1976.

Maps

AMERICAN LIBRARY ASSOCIATION. *Anglo-American Cataloging Rules: North American Text.* Chicago: ALA, 1970.

CAPPS, MARIE T. "Preservation and Maintenance of Maps," *Special Libraries*, LXIII (October, 1972): 457-62.

DRAZNIOWSKY, ROMAN. *Map Librarianship: Readings.* Metuchen, N.J.: Scarecrow Press, 1975.

FRIIS, HERMAN R. "Cartographic and Related Records: What Are They, How Have They Been Produced and What Are Problems of Their Administration?" *American Archivist*, XIII (April, 1950), 135-55.

GALNEDER, MARY. "Equipment for Map Libraries," *Special Libraries*, LXI (July-August, 1970), 271-74.

HILL, J. DOUGLAS. "Map and Atlas Cases," *Library Trends*, XIII (April, 1965), 481-87.

LE GEAR, CLARA. *Maps, Their Care, Repair and Preservation in Libraries.* Washington: Library of Congress, 1956.

MCDERMOTT, PAUL D. "What Is a Map?" *Journal of Geography*, LXVIII (November, 1969), 465-72.

POST, J. B. (ed.)., Map Librarianship, *Drexel Library Quarterly*, IX (October, 1973).

UNITED STATES. LIBRARY OF CONGRESS. SUBJECT CATALOGING DIVISION. *Classification, Class G: Geography, Maps, Anthropology, Recreation.* 4th ed. Washington: Government Printing Office, 1976.

WOLTER, JOHN A. "Research Tools and the Literature of Cartography," *AB Bookman's Yearbook*, Part I (1976), 21-30.

Photographs

BABCOCK, WILLOUGHBY M. "Some Sources for Northwest History: Cataloguing Pictorial Source Material," *Minnesota History*, XV (December, 1934), 439-44.

BETZ, ELISABETH W. "Organization and Cataloging of Pictorial Material in the Library of Congress Prints and Photographs Division." Unpublished manuscript, Library of Congress, 1978.

BOWDITCH, GEORGE. "Cataloging Photographs: A Procedure for Small Museums," *History News*, XXVI (November, 1971): 241-48.

HALLER, MARGARET. *Collecting Old Photographs.* New York: Arco Publishing Co., 1978.

HILL, DONNA. *The Picture File: A Manual and a Curriculum-Related Subject Heading List.* Hamden, Conn.: Linnet Book, 1975.

SHAW, RENATA V. "Picture Organization, Practices and Procedures, Part 1 and Part 2," *Special Libraries* (October, 1972): 322-43 and (November, 1972): 502-506.

VANDERBILT, PAUL. "Filing Systems for Negatives and Prints," *Complete Photographer*, V (1942), 1724-33.
_____. "Filing Your Photographs: Some Basic Procedures," *History News*, XXI (June, 1966), 117-24.
WEINSTEIN, ROBERT A., and BOOTH, LARRY. *Collection, Use, and Care of Historical Photographs.* Nashville: American Association for State and Local History, 1977.
WELLING, WILLIAM. *Collector's Guide to Nineteenth Century Photographs.* New York: Collier Books, 1976.

Planning for Users, Security and Space:
Reference

CONNOR, SEYMOUR V. "The Problem of Literary Property in Archival Depositories," *American Archivist*, XXI (April, 1958), 143-52.
EVANS, FRANK B. "The State Archivist and the Academic Researcher—'Stable Companionship,' " *American Archivist*, XXVI (July, 1963), 319-21.
JORDAN, PHILIP D. "The Scholar and the Archivist—A Partnership," *American Archivist*, XXXI (January, 1968), 57-65.
LAMB, W. KAYE. "The Archivist and the Historian," *American Historical Review*, LXVIII (January, 1963), 385-91.
PARKER, WYMAN W. "How Can the Archivist Aid the Researcher?" *American Archivist*, XVI (July, 1953), 233-40.
RUBINCAM, MILTON. "What the Genealogist Expects of an Archival Agency or Historical Society," *American Archivist*, XII (October, 1949), 333-38.
WINN, KARYL. "Common Law Copyright and the Archivist," *American Archivist*, XXXVII (July, 1974), 375-86.

Security

HAMILTON, CHARLES. "The Case of the Purloined Letters." In *Collecting Autographs and Manuscripts*, pp. 35-53. Norman: University of Oklahoma Press, 1968.
_____. *Scribblers and Scoundrels.* New York: P. S. Eriksson, 1968.
KINNEY, JOHN M. "Archival Security and Insecurity," *American Archivist*, XXXVIII (October, 1975), 493-97.
LAND, ROBERT H. "Defense of Archives Against Human Foes," *American Archivist*, XIX (April, 1956), 121-38.
MASON, PHILIP P. "Archival Security: New Solutions to an Old Problem," *American Archivist*, XXXVIII (October, 1975), 477-92.
SCOBEY, ALFREDA. "On Booknapping and Other Headaches," *Georgia Archive*, IV (Winter, 1976), 20-34.
TILLOTSON, ROBERT G. *Museum Security.* Paris: International Council of Museums, 1977.

Space

BARROW, WILLIAM J. "Archival File Folders," *American Archivist*, XXVIII (January, 1965), 125-28.
BARTKOWSKI, PATRICIA, and SAFFADY, WILLIAM. "Shelving and Other Furniture for Archives Buildings," *American Archivist*, XXXVII (January, 1974), 55-66.
CHRISTIAN, JOHN F., and FINNEGAN, SHONNIE. "On Planning an Archives," *American Archivist*, XXXVII (October, 1974), 573-78.
GONDOS, VICTOR, JR. "American Archival Architecture," *American Institute of Architects Bulletin*, I (Summer, 1947), 27-32.

MAUCK, VIRGINIA L. "Selection and Purchase of Archival Equipment and Supplies," *Illinois Libraries*, LIII (January, 1971), 18-21.

The Conservation and Preservation of Historical Materials:
Disaster Planning

BOHEM, HILDA. *Disaster Prevention and Disaster Preparedness*. Berkeley: University of California, 1978.

DONNELLY, R. R., and SONS, eds. *Florence Rises from the Flood*. Chicago: R. R. Donnelly and Sons Co., [1967]. Text by Harold Wtribolet and Joseph Judge.

HORTON, CAROLYN. "Saving the Libraries of Florence," *Wilson Library Bulletin*, XLI (June, 1967), 1034-43.

SPAWN, WILLMAN. "After the Water Comes," *Pennsylvania Library Association Bulletin*, XXVIII (1973), 243-51.

WATERS, PETER. *Procedures for Salvage of Water-damaged Library Material*. Washington: Library of Congress, 1972 (1975).

Paper Conservation

BAHMER, ROBERT H. "Recent American Developments in Archival Repair, Preservation and Photography," *Archivum*, X (1960), 59-71.

BANKS, PAUL N. "Environmental Standards for Storage of Books and Manuscripts," *Library Journal*, IC (February 1, 1974), 339-43.

BARROW, WILLIAM J.; VALINGER, LEON DE, JR.; and GEAR, JAMES L. "Lamination: A Symposium," *American Archivist*, XXVIII (April, 1965), 285-97.

CUNHA, GEORGE M., and CUNHA, DOROTHY G. *Conservation of Library Materials: A Manual and Bibliography on the Care, Repair, and Restoration of Library Materials*. 2 Vols. 2d ed. Metuchen, N.J.: Scarecrow Press, 1971.

CLAPP, ANNE F. *Curatorial Care of Works of Art on Paper*. Oberlin, Ohio: Intermuseum Conservation Association, 1973.

FRAZER, G. POOLE. "Some Aspects of the Conservation Problem in Archives," *American Archivist*, XL (April, 1977), 163-71.

HORTON, CAROLYN. *Cleaning and Preserving Bindings and Related Materials*. 2d rev. ed. Chicago: American Library Association, 1969.

SMITH, RICHARD D. "New Approaches to Preservation," *Library Quarterly*, XL (January, 1970): 139-71.

SPAWN, WILLMAN. "Physical Care of Books and Manuscripts." In *Book Collecting: A Modern Guide*, edited by Jean Peters, pp. 136-58. New York and London: R. R. Bowker Co., 1977.

UNITED STATES. LIBRARY OF CONGRESS. "Environmental Protection of Books and Related Materials." ("Preservation Leaflets," No. 2.) Washington: Library of Congress, 1975.

Bookbinding

GREATHOUSE, GLENN A., and WESSEL, CARL J., (eds.). *Deterioration of Materials*. New York: Reinhold Publishing Co., 1954.

HORTON, CAROLYN. *Cleaning and Preserving Bindings and Related Materials*. Chicago: American Library Association, 1967. ("LTP Publications," No. 12).

KATHPALIA, YASH PAL. *Conservation and Restoration of Archive Materials*. Paris: Unipub, 1974.

LANGWELL, WILLIAM H. *The Conservation of Books and Documents*. London: Sir Isaac Pitman and Sons, Ltd., 1957.

MUCCI, PAUL. *Paper and Leather Conservation: A Manual.* [College Park, Md.]: Mid Atlantic Regional Archives Conference, 1978.

PLENDERLEITH, HAROLD J. *The Conservation of Antiquities and Works of Art.* London: Oxford University Press, 1957.

WARDLE, D. B. *Document Repair.* London: Society of Archivists, 1971.